THE DARK INTERVAL

THE DARK
INTERVAL

TOWARDS A
THEOLOGY OF STORY

JOHN DOMINIC
CROSSAN

SONOMA, CALIFORNIA

Library of Congress Cataloging-in-Publication Data

Crossan, John Dominic.
 The dark interval.

 "Eagle books."
 Bibliography: p.
 Includes index.
  1. Literature—Philosophy. 2. Religion and
 literature. 3. Storytelling—Religious aspects—
 Christianity. I. Title.
 PN49.C7 1988   801'.9   88-12471
 ISBN 0-944344-06-2 (pbk.)

Printed in the United States of America

2   3   4   5   6   7   8   9   10

For my colleagues
in the Department of Religious Studies
at DePaul University, Chicago

I am the pause between two notes that fall
into a real accordance scarce at all:
for Death's note tends to dominate—

Both, though, are reconciled in the dark interval,
tremblingly.
And the song remains immaculate.

Rilke, *The Book of Hours*, 1

Contents

Foreword

The influence of this volume on biblical and theological scholarship has grown way out of proportion to its slender size. Its readership is attracted, in part, to the subject matter, and, in part, to the author's ability to cut through the haze of scholarship to the essence of matters. John Dominic Crossan's prose betrays its Irish roots and its poetic bent in almost every sentence. Yet style should not be allowed to obscure the significance of the topic: narrative in its various disguises.

This book attempts to isolate the parable as a type of story. Crossan compares and contrasts the parable to myth, apologue, action, and satire as other kinds of story telling. The parable, according to Crossan, lies on a spectrum of narrative possibilities that exhausts itself at either end: myth is located at one extreme, parable at the other. In order to establish this typology and the location of the parable, Crossan must do several things. It will perhaps not cripple the suspense of his sketch if we anticipate and formulate his goals in advance.

The author must first of all establish the limits of the spectrum. He must then locate myth at one end of the spectrum and show that myth is the polar opposite of parable. Crossan next analyzes the function of parable with the help of structuralism, which is a highly abstract way of correlating the structure of plot with the expectations of the listener/reader. Some of what he says in this connection sounds a bit dated in 1988, but is still very useful for his purposes. In any case, the structuralist features of his analysis do not overpower his fundamental argument. Finally, Crossan must test his proposal—his scheme, his paradigm—by detailed reference to Jesus' parables. This, in brief, is the outline of the book.

Since Crossan identifies myth and parable as lying at the outer limits of the spectrum at opposite ends, he must first demonstrate that story—and indeed all language—has limits. This is what he does in Chapter 1, "A Theology of Limit."

By establishing limits, Crossan prepares the way for transcendence. His closing remarks in the first chapter open directly onto this theme. It is appropriate that he do so since his entire book can be read as an apology for transcendence. If his book were narrative and if we were using his own paradigm, his work would therefore be classified as *apology*. It is an apology, although not in a narrative mode. This observation suggests that Crossan's typology may apply also to modes of language that are not narrative or not primarily narrative.

The ultimate limit is that human beings cannot get outside of story; we can get outside of particular stories, or particular forms of stories, but not outside of story as such. The world in which we live is a narrative world, created by and in our stories. We like to think that there is a world out there, quite concrete and objective and reliable, only to discover that that thought, too, is just another story. And so we go on proliferating stories in the vain hope that we will eventually arrive in some story that is quite literally and permanently and unalterably "true." The illusion that there is some final story that is eternally true is given expression in myth. The term myth is misleading in popular parlance. Myth does not mean a story that is not true, or a story that is about gods and goddesses; myths order the world in which we live by turning randomness into pattern, by replacing appearances with some ultimate reality, by reconciling the frustrations produced by contradictory experience in some higher unity. The basic function of myth is not the particular reconciliation established by individual myths; rather, its purpose is to establish that reconciliation is possible. Crossan puts it thus: It is more important to believe in the possibility of a solution than to find a specific one.

Myth creates worlds, quite literally, as suggested by the creation myths in Genesis 1 and 2. Parable, on the other hand, has the opposite function: Parable undercuts world; parable brings not peace but a sword. It does so by challenging the expectations raised in humankind by myth. Whatever we have come to expect, as a result of our myths, parable erodes, satirizes, explodes. If we think God will reward the good according to prevailing human standards, parables demonstrate the opposite. According to Crossan, parable attacks and subverts the received world; it is the dark night of story.

That is perhaps to make parable sound more ominous than it is, or at least than it appears. Parables do not always strike the hearer or reader as threatening. That is because listeners tend to attend the congenial and ignore what is strange; we steadily misread parables in accordance with our prevailing myths. But well constructed parables work against that powerful tendency in readers. They do so by undercutting our expectations so subtlety that we do not realize what has happened to us until it is too late.

All of this Crossan lays out in "The Ways of Story" and "The Tradition of Parable" (Chapters 2 and 3). And he does so with the aid of simple structural analyses and examples drawn from Ruth, Jonah, and the modern parable makers, Kafka and Borges. To put it in the simplest possible terms, as human beings we come to expect certain "givers" to give good gifts to certain "receivers," and to give bad gifts to certain other receivers. The good gifts might be designated O+ (a positive object), and the bad gifts O- (a negative object). Similarly, the good receivers can be termed R+ and the bad receivers R-. Myth has established and reinforces these expectations.

Imagine our surprise to find that O+ actually goes to R-, and O- to R+ in some particular story. The reversal makes that story a parable because it entails a reversal of expectations. Thus, Jonah, the prophet, disobeys God in the Book of Jonah, when we expect him, as a prophet, to obey God; and the people of Nineveh certainly disobey the divine command since in every form of the myth known to Israel that is the case; yet the Ninevites repent, much to everyone's surprise. The consequence is that Jonah is a parable since it reverses mythic expectations.

Crossan is particularly adept in sketching his understanding of the parables of Jesus in relation to this scheme. In this work and in his book, *In Parables*, he interprets the parables, and some acts of Jesus, as the powerful reversal of established expectations. For example, Jesus eats with sinners and prostitutes, when he, as a man of God, might be expected to socialize with respectable citizens. He

xii

reverses the validity of the prayers of the Pharisee and the Publican. And he makes the Samaritan out as a hero, when by rights he should have been the villain. He demonstrates, further, how the tradition in which these parables were embedded tends to deface their parabolic character and to reread them as myths, that is, as stories that reinforce the received world.

This proclivity of the tradition suggests the cycle through which traditions are wont to pass: myths establish and nourish a particular world in which contradictions and frustrations are reconciled; parables undermine that world by frustrating expectations and turning things upside down; parables then become domesticated in the traditions into which they pass and are turned once again into myths. A new parabler arises and then the cycle starts over again.

The movement of Crossan's book is also a cycle or a circle: he begins by establishing limits, and, at the end, he returns to the parable as limit. The parable is a fiction that calls attention to itself precisely as story and thus undercuts itself. Understood correctly, parable is its own limit.

Since in the words of Jesus the parable is about the Kingdom of God, it, too, must be some kind of limit. The Kingdom sets perpetual limits to human aspirations, to human expectations, and thereby frustrates them all. To his fellows Jesus seemed to be saying: whatever you hope for, whatever you want, whatever you think you should have—the kingdom is not that. It always comes as a surpise.

There are very difficult concepts to master in this brief volume. The unwary reader will come away frustrated, perhaps even angry. Yet the patient reader will find valuable clues to a profound understanding of the function of language, of story, of theology. He or she may even find that the understanding of the one is also the proper under-standing of the other. Crossan would have us think so.

In giving permission to reissue this work, Crossan has been good enough to go through the text and make certain corrections and additions. It is thus a revised or corrected edition. The editor has also undertaken to supplement the original bibliography, which was deliberately kept to the absolute minimum, with additional items. Crossan's work has some precursors and it has found many to follow out its numerous provocative leads. It seemed appropriate to surround the work with additional congenial company.

Robert W. Funk
Polebridge Press
The first day of spring, 1988

1

A
Theology
of Limit

I shall begin with a few comments explaining the word "limit" in order to remove its negative connotation. In talking about a theology of limit I am not saying that little seagulls should not learn to dive like falcons, if such be their pleasure. Neither am I talking of any form of limit which human malice invokes in order to subjugate or discriminate against another human being. And I am most emphatically not referring to any artificial limit set by arrogant human authority, be that arrogance racial or sexist, civil or ecclesiastical. And, finally, I am not interested in the limits of knowledge in the sense of what we do not know at present but which we will understand some time in the future.

What, then, do I intend by the invocation of limit? Two experiences above all. I am thinking first of our inevitable mortality, of that which was so hauntingly evoked in Rilke's magnificent "Ninth Elegy" from *The Duino Elegies:*

But because being here is much, and because
   all this
that's here, so fleeting, seems to require us
   and strangely
concerns us. Us the most fleeting of all.
   Just once,
everything, only for once. Once and no more.
   And we, too,
once. And never Again. But this
having been once, though only once,
having been once on earth—can it ever be cancelled?[1]

I quote precisely these lines because they face the inevitability of limitation, of life-towards-death, in the reiterated use of "once," yet they do not make it morbid or depressing. So, then, and first of all, I am speaking of the limit which is our mortality and of our inability to separate those twin features—life and death—in any fully human existence. Secondly, however, I am thinking of another limit which may well be much more profound than the limitation of death. Indeed, death may be only a sign and a reminder of this more fundamental limit. This is the limit of language, that is, *the limit which is language itself.* Our intentions, our theories, our visions are always confined within both language and story. A theology of limit seeks above all to explore this limitation which is posed by the inevitability of life within story, of existence in this story or that but always in some story. Such a theology might well take as its motto the aphorism of the philosopher Ludwig Wittgenstein that, "Man has the urge to thrust against the limits of language . . . but the tendency, the thrust, *points to something.*"[2]

1. Rilke, *Selected Works: II*, 244.
2. Waismann, "Notes," 12–13.

Game and Limit

Although this chapter will be primarily concerned with story, I intend to begin with game. The major reason is that we are accustomed and easily reconciled to limitation within game; we know how to distinguish the internal limit which is the game itself, with its established rules, from the external limit, which is simply our own ability or inability, our skill or our incompetence. It is with the internal rather than the external limitation that we are concerned here.

> *A man sat in a railroad station late at night. His train was long overdue. He finished his coffee and tried to decide where to place the empty Styrofoam cup on the floor. Not at his feet, surely, and not across the room, certainly. Finally he put it a few feet away, went back to his seat and began to toss the dime. Three hours later his train arrived. He had thrown the coin over a hundred times. He hand landed it in the cup exactly once.*

One feature of this whole process is very obvious. You notice it whenever you play a game. You tolerate a higher, even a total, failure rate more readily than you will tolerate a total or even high success rate. You yourself set up the rules and you therefore have set them up as you pleased. You fixed the limitations of distance against which you would test your aim. You would soon move the cup if you hit into it every time. But you might leave the cup in the same place and miss it a hundred times and still not give up the game.

A second instance. Imagine a room totally enclosed. It has no windows, and its door is so finely molded into the wall as to be almost invisible. Only some painted lines break the flat and absolute monotony of four walls, floor, and ceiling. Clear, precise, and perfect limits. If you are inside, must you feel enclosed and restricted? If it is a prison cell, the answer is presumably affirmative. Yet I spend a few hours of every week in a room like that and find its enclosed limitations exciting, exhilarating, and magnificently challenging. It is, of course, not a prison cell but a squash court. To play in and against such limits is not frustrating but refreshing.

Consider, then, a somewhat arbitrary distinction between game and sport. Let us use the word "sport" for competition in which individuals or teams oppose one another and in which there is always, even in overtime, a winner and a loser. And let us keep the term "game" for that process in which one individual or team competes against the limitations of possibility imposed by the rules themselves. For example, take golf, since it can easily be both game and sport in the above senses. As sport, it has winners and losers. But as game, it requires an individual to put a small white ball in a rather small hole in the ground in as few strokes as possible. That is supposed to be the theory, and when one makes a hole-in-one stroke it is considered a very special event. What would happen if somebody made a hole in one every time, with unerring inevitability? Would we not soon hear charges that it was no longer a game and that golf was being ruined? An individual, we might imagine, could still make a professional living on this accomplishment, but the ability would soon partake more of circus than of game. He would be considered more a freak than an athlete. Why is it, in other words, that game prohibits absolute success; that it allows and admires only partial and disciplined success, always mixed with failure? Paradoxically, perfect success in a game would be total failure, for then it would no longer be a game. To win absolutely would be to lose absolutely.

What does this strange trait of human nature tell us about ourselves? Why are we such creatures as make up games, inventing artificial rules and limits for ourselves and then straining against them to see how close we can come to beating those limits? But we do this in the certain knowledge that to beat the limits every time would be to destroy the game and so, in the very moment of victory, to achieve defeat? Why game?

I would suggest in answer that game is a very serious practice session for life and death, or, more precisely, for life towards death. It is a cautious experience of the necessity of limit and the inevitability of death. It is an experiment in disciplined failure. It is the joy of finitude and the laughter of limitation. We seek to avoid the deep challenge of game by talking only of sport and by talking mostly of winners. For in the final analysis we can only win against each other, we cannot win against the game. Only the game wins. Winners still lose to it. But notice one feature. Game teaches us to enjoy the limitation posed by the game itself. To destroy the limitation is to destroy the game. Imagine baseball with as many balls as the pitcher wanted and as many strikes as the batter chose.

This basic human experience of game opens the way for reflection on our necessary fascination with brinks and borders, with edges and limits.

Story and Limit

What about claims which deny the limitation of story and which hold, implicitly or explicitly, that we are capable of getting outside story to an objective reality? Three such claims have been extremely important in the formation of Western consciousness, and I must confess immediately that I can no longer believe in any of them, let alone in the combination of all three.

The first great master claim is one which makes a distinction between *art* (or faith, or imagination) and *science* (or fact, or reason) and then postulates for each a different language and a different destiny. Having established this complete disjunction, the claim then situates one term in hierarchical supremacy over the other. In our time, it is clear that for most people the ascendancy is that of science over art.

The second master claim is that of evolutionary *progress*—the claim that, if not every day and in every way, then at least some days and in some ways we are getting better and better. This is not taken merely as a story, a possible and most interesting way of seeing it, but as objective and realistic fact, open and obvious to the unprejudiced viewer.

The third master claim is the postulate that there is an external reality *out there*, extrinsic to our vision, our imagination, and our intellect and that we are gaining objective knowledge and disciplined control over this extramental reality.

All three claims can and do coalesce quite easily if, leaving aside art as inferior and ornamental, science is taken as pointing the way to progress as it increasingly comes to understand and control external reality. I admit that I can no longer believe in any of this. For now I accept a rather simple meaning in declaring these stories no longer true for me. The process philosopher Alfred North Whitehead stated it clearly. "In the real world, it is more important that a proposition be interesting than that it be true. The importance of truth is, that it adds to interest."[3] The same point is made by the Argentine writer Jorge Luis Borges in his short story "Death and the Compass." Two detectives discuss a recent murder. "'Possible but not interesting,' Lönnrot answered. 'You'll reply that reality hasn't the least obligation to be interesting. And I'll answer you that reality may avoid that obligation but that hypotheses may not.'"[4] So for now at least, when I say that these stories are not true, I mean no more than that they are no longer interesting. I am sure that if I were pushed to explain and defend the term "interesting" I would say that the most interesting story for me is that which best opens up the possibility of transcendental experience for here and now. Let us have some witnesses, then, against these three claims that deny their own being as story and maintain that they are telling us how it really is and not how I-you-we-they have agreed to imagine it. In the process of presenting these witnesses I hope to make clear more precisely what I mean by the limits of story and by story as limit.

Art and Science

In this section I am bringing together two somewhat unlikely partners, the philosopher Ludwig Wittgenstein and the novelist C. P. Snow. I am interested in what happens when one opens up a metaphysical distinction between art and science, between the language of poetry and the language of physics. Even if the distinction is made in order to exalt art over science, as with Wittgenstein, it can just as easily be used to elevate science over art, as with Snow. In order to avoid this latter

3. Whitehead, *Process and Reality*, 303.
4. Borges, "Death and the Compass," 77.

hierarchy, one may have to qualify very carefully the exact dimensions of the distinction. We know all too well in the contemporary world that precisely how one distinguishes, say, female from male or black person from white person may establish already the hierarchy one wishes to claim for one over the other.

There was once a man who owned some property on a high cliff which overlooked the sea. He spent many years of careful construction on a road from his house to the very edge of the cliff. When the road was finished, he spent hours each day standing on the extreme edge where he could feel the thrill of the sea. The people who lived round about were practical and sensible folk, and they said that he was a very good roadbuilder and that he certainly liked to walk a lot.

At the very beginning and again at the end of his *Tractatus Logico-Philosophicus* the (not so) British philosopher Ludwig Wittgenstein placed the cryptic aphorism, "Whereof one cannot speak, thereof one must be silent."[5] This saying was clearly of great significance for him, as both its repetition and its framing position would indicate. And its gnomic nature was such that one could hardly blame commentators if they misconstrued its thrust. They took it completely for granted that he was saying we should not talk of such things as art or ethics or theology because these things simply do not exist; they refer to no objectively verifiable referential object. The commentators should have remembered, however, one very interesting episode prior to Wittgenstein's departure from Vienna to England. When he was finally persuaded to speak to the Vienna Circle of philosophers, he chose to read them

5. Wittgenstein, *Tractatus Logico-Philosophicus*, Preface and #7.

poetry rather than lecture them on philosophy. In any case, here is the difference between Wittgenstein and the positivists, according to Paul Engelmann.

A whole generation of disciples was able to take Wittgenstein as a positivist, because he has something of enormous importance in common with the positivists: he draws the line between what we can speak about and what we must be silent about just as they do. The difference is only that they have nothing to be silent about. . . . Positivism holds—and this is its essence—that what we can speak about is all that matters in life. *Whereas Wittgenstein passionately believes that all that really matters in human life is precisely what, in his view, we must be silent about.* . . . When he nevertheless takes immense pains to delimit the unimportant [i.e., the scope and limits of ordinary language], it is not the coastline of that island which he is bent on surveying with such meticulous accuracy, but the boundary of the ocean.[6]

The thesis that Wittgenstein was interested in the boundary of the dry land (science) because of the excitement of the ocean bordering upon it (art) can be proved convincingly from some of his own letters of that period. There is something ironically sad in reading his letter to Bertrand Russell, who had sponsored him in his new country. He informs Russell that his enthusiasm for the *Tractatus* is misplaced and that he has completely misunderstood it. Wittgenstein distinguishes between what can be explained in the clear and logical propositions of scientific language and what can only be shown in indirect and poetic ways. (This includes such vital areas as ethics, for

6. Janik and Toulmin, *Wittgenstein's Vienna*, 191, 220, 191.

example). The key passage is worth quoting: "Now I am afraid you haven't really got hold of my main contention, to which the whole business of logical propositions is only a corollary. The main point is the theory of what can be explained by propositions—i.e., by language . . . and what cannot be expressed by propositions, but only shown; which I believe, is the cardinal problem of philosophy."[7] In a letter to Ficker he made his purpose even clearer.

> *The book's point is an ethical one.* I once meant to include in the preface a sentence which is not in fact there now; but which I will write out for you here, because it will perhaps be a key to the work for you. What I meant to write, then, was this: My work consists of two parts: the one presented here plus all that I have *not* written. And *it is precisely that second part that is the important one.* My book draws limits to the sphere of the ethical from the inside as it were, and I am convinced that this is the only rigorous way of drawing those limits.[8]

It might have made quite a difference to have had that sentence in the preface but, again, possibly not, for one sees what one wants in such cases. Why is that man standing on the edge of the cliff? Is the cliff where the land ends or where the waters begin?

Wittgenstein intended to delineate the edges of ordinary, descriptive language, within which science and logic could operate, and, at the same time, to indicate the areas outside ordinary language where questions of ethics, values, and ultimate meanings are known in mystical intuition and conveyed ("shown") in the indirect and

7. Fann, *Wittgenstein's Conception of Philosophy*, 22.
8. Janik and Toulmin, *Wittgenstein's Vienna*, 192.

metaphorical language of poetry and art. But even if he believed that what could be *shown* in art was much more important than what could be *spoken* in science, it is immediately obvious that, with the distinction once established, the hierarchical priority can be argued just as well for science over art as for art over science.

And that is precisely the clear and unequivocal conclusion of C. P. Snow, looking back years later on his famous book, *Two Cultures*. What is most fascinating in his comments in the *Times Literary Supplement* is the sheer arrogance of his language and his comparisons. The language is as prejudicial as if one were to divide people into male and nonmale, races into white and nonwhite, or religions into Christian and non-Christian. Notice in the following paraphrase how science is always defined in first place and with positive qualities while art is always in second place and defined as the mere negation of those qualities postulated for science. I shall paraphrase his statements but keep this subtle imperialism.

There are, Snow claimed, two kinds of understanding, two ways of dealing with experience—there really are two, and only two. He first describes the way of science as a search for agreement which builds brick by brick, incorporating what has been previously done into the growing structure. The article proceeds with subtle linguistic discrimination to identify "the other way of knowing" as the mere negation of the first way. This second way, the humanist culture, is such that we will always have to go back and read, for example, Shakespeare and Tolstoy. The creators and creations of humanist culture have not passed, and cannot pass, into a general agreement or a collective mind. Snow's conclusion makes the humanist culture pale before the scientific culture. "So we seem to have reached a clear divide between two cultures or traditions. One is cumulative, incorporative, collective, consensual, so designed that it must progress through time. The other is non-cumulative, non-incorporative, unable to abandon its part but also unable to embody it. . . . it loses by its nature the diachronic progress which is science's greatest gift to the mind of man."[9]

Without any doubt this is the popular viewpoint on science, and most ordinary people will not question it, especially when "science" means, for example, medicine. Again, notice the order of description, with science first and art second, and the positive qualities of science, art being described only through the negations of these positive gifts. And notice especially the combination, in the last sentence, of science and progress.

This statement by Snow (science over art) is clearly opposed to Wittgenstein's intention (art over science), but it brings home the problem most forcibly. And the problem is not the propriety of the hierarchy, one way or the other, but the very validity of the distinction itself. The most basic question for a theology of limit and of story is whether there is any such direct, ordinary, objective, descriptive language as over against some other type, whether it is considered to be a higher or a lower type. To concede objectivity to scientific language is to lose the battle before the first shot is fired. One will never prevail on such a field. But it may well be that there is only indirect (if you will excuse the redundancy) language. In that case the real distinction would not be between the direct language of science and the indirect language of poetry but between language, whether in science or in poetry or in anything else, which is aware of its limits and

9. Snow, in *London Times Literary Supplement*, 9 July 1970.

language when it is fossilized and totally oblivious to the yawning chasm beneath its complacency. Art and science may not be two simultaneous and parallel ways of knowing, but art and science may be, and in that order, two successive moments of any truly human knowledge. We will return to this point in considering the third master claim later on.

Evolutionary Progress

Next comes the great master claim of the Western world, that of progress. It is a claim so profound and pervasive that it surfaces in such disparate places as the utopian socialism of Karl Marx and the Christian eschatology of Teilhard de Chardin. Indeed, the former thinker found it much easier to be rid of faith in God than of hope in progress. Which makes one wonder, in passing, if that God had any other major function besides being guarantor for that progress. The great Western claim is of the past and future progress of the human race. We have in our vocabulary a neutral word such as "change" and we have also words such as "improvement" and "decline." These two add to change the idea of for-the-better or for-the-worse. "Evolution" has been taken for a hundred years, not as a neutral word denoting change, but as a positive word implying improvement. This improvement is taken to be so self-evident that the only way to offset its claim is to be deliberately perverse and argue that the human race is steadily declining and that evolution is slow deterioration.

Against this claim of progress and evolutionary improvement I would bring certain witnesses for change without progress and for evolution without improvement. I would not be misunderstood; it is not evolution I wish to dispute but the claim of progress therein. Once again I shall be working with art and science as the poles of the discussion.

I shall begin with art because it was in art and poetry, in architecture and drama, that I first saw most clearly the total lack of any evolutionary progress. Change, by all means, but improvement?

What happens when a modern person stands before cave paintings over fifteen thousand years old? Does one really think, Well, not bad, considering their stage of evolution? Can one talk of artistic progress at all? In the summer of 1919 the poet T. S. Eliot visited the Dordogne caves in southern France and saw what a Magdalenian artist had done with magnesium oxide and buffalo grease on an Upper Paleolithic wall. Years later Eliot drew two conclusions from that experience, one on art and one on humanity. In a 1932 essay he stated them in a sentence which became something of an aphorism: "art never improves, but . . . the material of art is never quite the same."[10] There is, of course, and quite obviously, change in art, but "this change is a development which abandons nothing *en route*, which does not superannuate either Shakespeare, or Homer, or the rock drawing of the Magdalenian draughtsmen."[11] This takes art, at least, out of any scheme of evolutionary progress because "this development, refinement perhaps, complication certainly, is not, from the point of view of the artist, any improvement."[12] In a second essay, published that same year, this intuition concerning art was widened to apply to both humanity and holiness: "And we must affirm that perfection is as nearly attainable for man here and now as it ever

10. Eliot, "Tradition and the Individual Talent," 261.
11. "Tradition and the Individual Talent," 261.
12. "Tradition and the Individual Talent," 261.

will be in any future in any place. That there can be no art greater than the art which has already been created: there will only be different and necessarily different combinations of the eternal and changing in the forms of art."[13] There is a bite in all this, however, which makes either complacency or despair impossible. If it is true that Chartres cathedral was, is, and ever will be a work of consummate art, it is equally true and even more devastatingly obvious that we cannot build a Chartres today. One does not triumph over or even improve upon past artistic greatness. It is enough to be as great. Or, as Eliot himself wrote in "East Coker,"

> There is only the fight to recover what has been lost
> And found and lost again and again: and now, under
>   conditions
> That seem unpropitious. But perhaps neither gain nor
>   loss.
> For us, there is only the trying. The rest is not our
>   business.[14]

This example from art is important enough to stay with for a few moments. I have argued that the history of art shows no evolutionary progress (or decline, either) across the centuries. Yet it is certainly obvious that art has not been either static or moribund throughout these same centuries. Therefore, we have movement without progress, we have change without improvement. This does not mean that at any given moment there may not be good or bad, better or worse, in art but that if one tried to make a graph of its history, over the centuries, the graph would look, I suppose, rather like a person's electrocardiogram. It would

13. Eliot, "A Commentary," 78.
14. Eliot, *Four Quartets,* 31.

15

not be a clear, rising line, but neither would it be a circle closed in on itself. The question, then, is whether such a graph might not be a master paradigm for all human activities, not just for art.

C. P. Snow used precisely this nonprogress of art to argue for its inferiority to the clear progress of science. But, as against a popular propagandist such as Snow, the historians and philosophers of science raise very disturbing questions about this progress which has been claimed as almost synonymous with science itself.

In his fascinating book *The Structure of Scientific Revolutions*, Thomas S. Kuhn dismisses this theory of steady and cumulative progress on the part of science by drawing attention to the master paradigms which control such cumulative progress.[15] There may be clear and steady progress within any given overarching theory or paradigm, but where would you stand to compare such overarching theories with one another? And what of master paradigms that nobody thought of and for which it is now too late? I would presume, for example, in 1975, that all of us are no longer as sure as we once were that a way of life based on unlimited and fairly cheap oil is the best of all possible worlds, the manifest path of destiny and progress.

When a master paradigm breaks down and another takes its place, the latter is not derived by logical deduction from the ruins of the preceding paradigm or model. The people who know this all too well are the scientists who have created a scientific revolution. A classic example by Russell Kirk records the delight of Albert Einstein as the poet St.-John Perse explained to him the importance of intuition in poetry. "'But it's the same thing for the man of

15. Kuhn, *The Structure of Scientific Revolutions*, 126.

16

science,' he said. 'The mechanics of discovery are neither logical nor intellectual. It's a sudden illumination, almost a rapture. Later, to be sure, intelligence analyzes and experiments confirm (or invalidate) the intuition. But initially there is a great forward leap of the imagination.'"[16]

This makes the moment when master paradigms are created in science look similar to the great visionary intuitions of the poet. It also makes one wonder if Eliot's phrase might not be just as true of science as it is of art: "science never improves, but the material of science is never the same."

The French anthropologist Claude Lévi-Strauss seems to be saying this in a discussion of the "Neolithic Paradox." "It was in neolithic times that man's mastery of the great arts of civilization—of poetry, weaving, agriculture and the domestication of animals—became firmly established. No one today would any longer think of attributing these enormous advances to the fortuitous accumulation of a series of chance discoveries or believe them to have been revealed by the passive perception of certain natural phenomena."[17] In other words, when we look at this list of discoveries made over ten thousand years ago, we can only conclude that, "Neolithic, or early historical, man was therefore the heir of a long scientific tradition."[18] It did not all happen by chance or coincidence. Somebody hypothesized, experimented, and concluded.

But if we grant that neolithic *science* was worthy of this name, how do we explain the difference between it and modern science? Lévi-Strauss suggests that there are two distinct modes of scientific thought. But he argues that "these are certainly not a function of different stages of

16. Kirk, *Eliot and His Age*, 142.
17. Levi-Strauss, *The Savage Mind*, 13–14.
18. Levi-Strauss, *The Savage Mind*, 15.

development of the human mind but rather of two strategic levels at which nature is accessible to scientific inquiry: one roughly adapted to that of perception and the imagination: the other at a remove from it."[19] His example of this difference has become something of a classic. The neolithic scientist is like the handyman who can fix anything by clever adaptation of the materials at hand. The modern scientist will study the problem in the abstract, define the solution, and order the needed materials to be made from appropriate supplies of their raw state. In the final analysis, the difference may come down to counting in one's head as against counting on one's very concrete fingers. Our science, precisely as science, is not better than neolithic science. It is simply different. If one insists that modern science is both different and better, it might be as well to remember that the bill for modern science has not yet been paid in full. We do know that neolithic science did not destroy the earth or render its climate unlivable. So let us settle for difference rather than progress between neolithic and modern science, and let us hope we are as creative as humans then were, and at no greater cost to our humanity or the earth's well-being.

If evolutionary *progress* is simply a piece of major Western arrogance, does that mean our life becomes meaningless, a boring repetition of repetitious boredom? Stand on the shore and look at the sea. Is it boring, is it ever boring? Yet, there it is, motion without progress, forever.

Here are two passages from Ezra Pound's "Canto 81." The first reminds us to think twice before we concoct claims of progress with ourselves as its present peak.

19. Levi-Strauss, *The Savage Mind*, 15.

The ant's a centaur in his dragon world.
Pull down thy vanity, it is not man
Made courage, or made order, or made grace,
    Pull down thy vanity, I say pull down.[20]

The second passage reassures us that the abandonment of this claim is superiority over all that has preceded us need not in any way diminish our humanity.

But to have done instead of not doing
        this is not vanity
To have, with decency, knocked
That a Blunt should open
    To have gathered from the air a live tradition
or from a fine old eye the unconquered flame
This is not vanity.
    Here error is all in the not done,
    all in the diffidence that faltered.[21]

It is enough, it is sublimely enough, to do as well as the best of the past, and it will strain our every effort to do just that.

External Reality

The problem is so obvious it is difficult to see, like something too close to my eyes. For example, if I wore red sunglasses the world would look red to me. But I could take them off and see that it was actually multicolored. Even if I never took them off, others, not wearing them, would tell me of the world's color spectrum. But suppose *everyone* had red contact lenses physically molded to their eyes, and nobody knew that the lenses were present. Then

20. Pound, *The Cantos of Ezra Pound*, 521–22.
21. Pound, *The Cantos of Ezra Pound*, 521–22.

19

would everyone be in complete agreement that the world was red? Not really. Nobody would say "red"; they would say the world was the way it was. Unless, of course, somebody said one day: "What if we all have red contact lenses?" and so on. What I am getting at is this: Do we (or does society or family or church for us) first propose theories and then try to see if the "facts" fit them, or do we first see the facts out there and propose theories to account for them? Which comes first, the theory or the fact?

I shall begin with another quotation from Thomas S. Kuhn's book because it catches beautifully the ambivalence all of us feel when first confronted with this problem.

Is sensory experience fixed and neutral? Are theories simply man-made interpretations of given data? The epistemological viewpoint that has most often guided Western philosophy for three centuries dictates an immediate and unequivocal, Yes! In the absence of a developed alternative, I find it impossible to relinquish entirely that viewpoint. Yet it no longer functions effectively, and the attempts to make it do so through the introduction of a neutral language of observation is now seen to be hopeless.[22]

Kuhn states that this is the way we have been trained to answer that question: the data, the facts are out there; we should/could observe them neutrally and objectively and make up theories to explain them impartially and without prejudice.

The English philosopher of science, Karl Popper, goes beyond this ambivalence and argues flatly that theory precedes observation, but he also admits the difficulty.

22. Kuhn, *The Structure of Scientific Revolutions*, 126.

20

"The belief that science proceeds from observation to theory is still so widely and firmly held that my denial of it is often met with incredulity. . . . But in fact the belief that we can start with pure observation alone, without anything in the nature of a theory, is absurd."[23]

Another philosopher of science, Mary Hesse, makes a similar point, but she also draws attention to the role of society in all of this. "Contrary to what some empiricist philosophers seem to have held, 'observation-descriptions' are not written on the face of events to be transferred directly into language but are already 'interpretations' of events, and the kind of interpretation depends on the framework of assumptions of a language community."[24] We have usually been told the theories and the facts that "proved them." This was, of course, highly persuasive since the theory also taught us what was and was not a "fact." It is only when we imagine other theories and wonder how different the "facts" might then be, that we see the problem for the first time.

All of which serves to destroy Snow's "two ways of knowing" and the superiority of the scientific over the humanistic way. We begin to see instead a much closer relationship between the paradigms of the scientist and the visions of the poet or artist. We also realize that while there can certainly be progress within a given paradigm, and while there are certainly changes of paradigms, there may well be no progress and improvement of paradigms as such. But we also see emerging here a far more disquieting theory than one which postulated "two ways" of knowing, however hierarchically arranged they were to be. For the poet and for the scientist alike, reality is not

23. Popper, *Conjectures and Refutations*, 46.
24. Hesse, *Models and Analogies in Science*, 15.

something objectively "out there" about which we are getting more and more exact knowledge.

One final example: The critic Christine Brooke-Rose says,

> The facts can only be the facts as apprehended by man, and these do alter considerably when a working hypothesis (e.g., Newton's), which worked for a long time, is upset by a new equation or a new working hypothesis (e.g., Einstein's), just as Einstein's theory has been to a certain extent modified by Heisenberg. Even the principle that the observed thing is altered by the instrument observing it is nearer to the artistic than to any old-fashioned mechanistic view.[25]

At this point it does look like something beyond idealism or realism is at work, something which might be termed relativism, if that word were not already reprobate. If it will not abuse the language too much we might call this new theory "relationism." Reality is neither *in here* in the mind nor *out there* in the world; it is the interplay of both mind and world in language. Reality is relational and relationship. Even more simply, reality is language. What is there before us and is without language is as unknowable as the answer to the question of how we would feel had we never been born. The Bible suggests (one of its less happy suggestions) that we go to the ant and learn its ways. A better suggestion would be to go to the spider and study its destiny and ponder how it weaves a web from inside itself and then dwells in it and calls it world (I suppose). All of which means we had better take language very carefully and treat our poets very seriously.

As Plato knew long ago, poets are the dangerous ones.

25. Brooke-Rose, *A ZBC of Ezra Pound*, 123.

There is no such thing as an innocent poem, and the most dangerous are not those which question national policy or political purpose but those which make us question perception itself. It all looks so terribly simple. The poet talks about the rose. But, we say, she is not really talking about the rose as it really is but about her relationship to the rose and the rose in relationship to herself. And that, we add swiftly and glibly, is what distinguishes poetry from the rest of language because with other language we are describing things as they are and not our relationship to them and theirs to us. Of course. Unless, maybe, ...

If there is only language, and if being human means living in language and calling that process reality, we can listen anew to the poets whose claims may not seem as extravagant now as before—three American poets, for example.

In his essay, "The Constant Symbol," Robert Frost pleads for the view that "poetry is simply made of metaphor. So also is philosophy—and science, too, for that matter, if it will take the soft impeachment from a friend."[26] Once an artistic or scientific revolution has taken place and we look backwards, we usually find the whole progress logical and even necessary. This is inevitable since we now see the past in the light of the present, the old in the light of the new. But what we never know and never can know, after an Einstein has given us a post-Newtonian vision, is what other vision, what alternative to Einstein never made it to Bethlehem to be born. A second example: Northrop Frye has summed up the theory and practice of Wallace Stevens in one sentence: "The motive for metaphor, according to Wallace Stevens, is a desire to associate, and finally to identify, the human

26. Frost, *Critical Essays*, 128.

mind with what goes on outside it, because the only genuine joy you can have is in those rare moments when you feel that although we may know in part, as Paul says, we are also a part of what we know."[27] Or, to play with Paul some more, we do not mourn that we see through a glass darkly, we now rejoice in the dark loveliness of the glass. Black is beautiful. Finally, over twenty-five years ago the poet William Carlos Williams, in his essay "An Approach to the Poem," gave us a litmus test by which we can determine whether we still prefer to live in the story of reality-out-there or are ready for a sterner challenge. Do we find the following statement acceptable? "Until your artists have conceived you in your unique and supreme form you can never conceive yourselves, and have not, in fact, existed."[28]

Limit and Transcendence

The main objection I have been making to the three claims just studied is that they do not consider themselves as stories, as possible ways of imagining, but as objective and neutral descriptions of how reality is. If I accept them as stories, which is the way I actually see them, my only objection to them is that they have become boring, uninteresting, and in direct conflict with some more challenging and exciting new stories. The only thing that is "wrong" with them is what was "wrong" with classical art when modern art had arrived on the scene. I propose, then, to consider as most interesting the story that art and science, or poetic intuition and scientific achievement, are not two simultaneous and separate ways of knowing but

27. Frye, *The Educated Imagination*, 33.
28. Williams, "An Approach to the Poem," 60.

24

two successive and connected moments of all human knowledge; that there is continual evolutionary change but no overall evolutionary progress; and that "reality" is the world we create in and by our language and our story so that what is "out there," apart from our imagination and without our language, is as unknowable as, say, our fingerprints, had we never been conceived. To ask, in other words, what is "out there" apart from the story in which "it" is envisioned, should strike us as strangely as would the question of how one might feel today about the fact that one had never been born. I am not saying we cannot know reality. I am claiming that what we know is reality, is our reality here together and with each other.

Having absolutely limited myself within a story, whether this, that, or some other story, I do not feel constrained or confined because, as with my earlier analogy of game, I find that limitation exhilarating.

All of which brings me to the following problem. If there is only story, then God, or the referent of transcendental experience, is either inside my story and, in that case, at least in the Judeo-Christian tradition I know best, God is merely an idol I have created; or, God is outside my story, and I have just argued that what is "out there" is completely unknowable. So it would seem that any transcendental experience has been ruled out, if we can only live in story. In all of this I admit most openly a rooted prejudice against worshipping my own imagination and genuflecting before my own mind.

The Death of the Lighthouse Keeper

Once upon a time there were people who lived on rafts upon the sea. The rafts were constructed of materials from the land whence they had come. On this land was a lighthouse in which there was a lighthouse keeper. No

25

matter where the rafts were, and even if the people themselves had no idea where they actually were, the keeper always knew their whereabouts. There was even communication between people and keeper so that in an absolute emergency they could always be guided safely home to land.

In rather crude form that is the story in which the classical mind dwelt brilliantly for centuries. It was, again, a very good story and a very interesting one. One could, for example, call the lighthouse keeper God, if one were so inclined. And even if one did not want to do anything as embarrassingly honest as that, one could have brilliant methodological doubts about rafts and winds and currents because, no matter how much one doubted, the light-house keeper knew the answer, and his knowledge was known as truth. Then one day the rumor came that destroyed the classical vision. It did not say that the lighthouse keeper had died and that the lighthouse was in ruins, its light gone out forever; it said that there was no dry land, so how could there be either a lighthouse or a lighthouse keeper? The rumor's most cogent articulation is usually attributed to the poet-philosopher Nietzsche, whose madman announced to the startled villagers that mankind had murdered God. The announcer, for all his madness, was well aware of the vertiginous terror of the event he proclaimed.

All of us are his murderers. But how have we done this? How were we able to drink up the sea? Who gave us the sponge to wipe away the entire horizon? What did we do when we unchained this earth from its sun? Whither is it moving now? Whither are we moving now? Away from all suns? Are we not plunging continually? Backward, sideward, forward, in all directions? Is there any up or down left? Are we not straying as through an infinite nothing?[29]

That is one version of the rumor, but I have always preferred another and equally early version of it. The reason is purely personal. It is that Emily Dickinson makes me shiver in a way that Nietzsche has never been able to do. Her version:

Finding is the first Act
The second, loss,
Third, Expedition for
the "Golden Fleece."

Fourth, no Discovery —
Fifth, no Crew —
Finally, no Golden Fleece —
Jason — sham — too.[30]

In that "sham" one hears the chilling slam as the door closes on the classical vision of a fixed center out there somewhere. What had died was the fixed center outside language, and for many who attended the funeral that could only mean the burial of God since they equated the two. When one believed in a fixed reality out there, apart from us and independent of us, one could easily imagine God as the one who really knew all about it. It was God's knowledge of it that made it what it *really* was, and we could easily imagine ourselves knowing more and more about it so that even if *our* knowledge was all wrong, God at least knew the correct answer. In fact, if we could get God on our side, would not progress be assured and inevitable since we would be seeing reality more and more

29. Nietzsche, *The Portable Nietzsche*, 95.
30. Dickinson, *The Poems of Emily Dickinson*, 2:647–48, #870.

as God saw it? Yet who would need such a God if reality was not outside us but inside our language? So, with the loss of credibility in a fixed reality independent of us, there soon followed the loss of faith in a God whose chief role was to guarantee that reality's validity.

The Renewal of Transcendence

For those who could not or would not accept the presumption that the shift from the classical to the modern mind (change, not improvement!), which necessarily meant the loss of the fixed center's security, necessarily meant also the death of God, there was work to be done. T. S. Eliot hurried home from the funeral of the lighthouse keeper and challenged us, in "Ash Wednesday," to:

> Redeem
> The time, Redeem
> The unread vision in the higher dream
> While jewelled unicorns draw by the
> gilded hearse.[31]

Let us try, then, a second version of the story that appeared earlier.

There is no lighthouse keeper. There is no lighthouse. There is no dry land. There are only people living on rafts made from their own imaginations. And there is the sea.

(It was still there, Emily, even with Jason gone). Why might it not be possible to experience transcendence now from the call of the sea, as once before from the voice of the lighthouse keeper?

One moment. If there are only rafts and these rafts are really language itself, what is this sea which is "outside"

31. Eliot, *The Complete Poems*, 64.

28

language because it is beyond the raft? Maybe there is no
sea either? If there is only language, then God must be
either inside language and in that case, as I said above, an
idol; or he is outside language, and there is nothing out
there but silence. There is only one possibility left, and
that is what we can experience in the movement of the
raft, in the breaks in the raft's structure, and, above all,
what can be experienced at the *edges* of the raft itself. For
we cannot really talk of the sea, we can only talk of the
edges of the raft and what happens there. Our prayer will
have to be, not "Thank God for edges," but "Thank edges
for God."

The French philosopher Paul Ricoeur may have had
something like this in mind when he said that there was
no mystery *in* language but only the mystery *of* language.[32] There are no mysteries on the raft but, as Galileo
might have said, still it moves. At this point one can also
appreciate why the American scholar Paul Van Buren has
written a philosophy of religion with the title *The Edges of
Language*. In summary, the classical mind says, that's only
a story, but the modern mind says, there's only story.

A concluding analogy. For myself at least, the most
exciting way to sail a boat is on a close-haul course,
beating as close to the eye of the wind as possible. The
limitation is absolute. One cannot sail into the eye of the
wind any more, I would argue, than one can get outside
language and outside story. But one can sail as close as
possible into the wind, and one can tell that one is as close
as possible only by constantly testing the wind. Then the
boat heels over, strains hard, and one experiences most
fully, or at least I do, the thrill of sailing. My suggestion is
that the excitement of transcendental experience is found

32. Ricoeur, "The Problem of the Double-Sense," 79.

only at the edge of language and the limit of story and that the only way to find that excitement is to test those edges and those limits. And that, as we shall see, is what parable is all about.

2

The
Ways
of Story

In the last chapter I argued the proposition that we live in story like fish in the sea. It does not at all trouble me to contemplate the inevitability that this too must be a story, because it is the story in which I now have to live, and I know that in this I am not alone. I am quite aware that there are other master stories around, and to those who can live in them I can only wish that they both fare forward and fare well. I find my story different and presently necessary, and I also find that I need to claim no more for it than that. That will suffice.

The next step, then, having taken the necessity of story as our present master story, is to investigate the ways of story and especially to pursue the question of how God can be experienced in such a situation.

In this chapter I shall be discussing various ways in story, but the major emphases will be on *myth* and on *parable* as the poles of story. In defining these terms as the limits of story's possibilities I shall be using them in a strict and technical sense which will, I hope, become clearer as we proceed. This attempt at mapping the edges of story operates in definite consciousness of the warning of Northrop Frye that "The poet's function is still his primitive oral function of defining and illustrating the concerns of the society that man is producing, but this fact is not generally realized. It is not realized partly because the language of poetry is still thought of as a rhetorical and sublogical language: the principles of mythical language are still largely unknown."[1] Careful cartography, then, is in order.

Myth as Reconciliation

To begin with, two negatives: "Myth" is not used here in its ordinary popular usage as synonymous with sophisticated lying. Neither is it used to mean stories with gods and goddesses in them, simply because such personalities appear in the stories. The guide for our discussion will be Claude Lévi-Strauss, whose brilliant structural analyses of myths have offered a far sharper definition for the word than either of these two popular conceptions.

The Structure of Myth

The Academy Award for best leading male actor was voted to Marlon Brando in 1973. He refused the Oscar, and a Native American actress appeared in his place to explain that his refusal was in protest against the denigration of the Native American in Hollywood westerns. He was not protesting any individual movie but a *pattern* which emerged with repeated and relentless inevitability from the entire corpus of "cowboys and Indians" films. It was a pattern that every role-playing child knew so in-

1. Frye, "The Critical Path," 297.

stinctively that "I don't want to be the Indian" became a standard objection in children's play. The protest was aimed at what we might term a *structure of contempt* which was built into the entire portrayal of Native Americans on film.

This example helps our understanding of what Lévi-Strauss seeks as he investigates a vast repertoire of myth. He is not looking at the surface story for itself, however exciting that may be, nor at the actors and their roles, however fascinating these may be. He is looking for the structure, at the deepest level possible. In order to get at this deep structure without getting lost in the multitudinous variations of surface adventure, Lévi-Strauss must concentrate on the relations, indeed on the *bundles of relations*, between the units of the myth. For instance, imagine that somebody challenged the Oscar protest and denied that there was a structure of contemptuous chauvinism within Hollywood's "Indian" movies. Suppose we responded that in many "Indian" films there is a beautiful "Indian" girl who helps the white hero, even betraying her own people for his love, and who is then killed off, usually heroically and self-sacrificially, to avoid the specter of miscegenation at the end. If one wished to show the white male chauvinism in this pattern, one would have to argue not from one instance in one film, which might even be historically accurate, but from the *bundles of relations* within a whole series of films. The chauvinism cannot be proved from the relation of *one* "Indian" girl to *one* white man in *one* movie. Only the bundles or sets of such relations in as many movies as possible will prove it—and then with a compelling precision. With Lévi-Strauss, we are seeking the structure of bundles of relations in myths. From one example comes only a sequence: "Indian" girl dies to save white man from death. From many examples comes a structure (and an ideology): "Indian" girl must die to save society from miscegenation. That is why Lévi-Strauss's seminal article of 1955, "The Structural Study of Myth," which has since appeared in his collection *Structural Anthropology*, concludes that "the question has often been raised why myths, and more generally oral literature, are so addicted to duplication, triplication, or quadruplication of the same sequence. If our hypotheses are accepted, the answer is obvious: The function of repetition is to render the structure of the myth apparent."[2]

Lévi-Strauss is not concerned with only one collection of myths, although one such series is, of course, his area of specific illustration and concentration. He is really interested in the structure of myth as such, if not, indeed, with the structure of the mind as such. What, then, is the structure of myth as myth?

The English anthropologist, Edmund Leach, has summarized Lévi-Strauss succinctly: "So, despite all variations . . . this aspect of myth is a constant. In every myth system we will find a persistent sequence of binary discriminations as between human/superhuman, mortal/immortal, male/female, legitimate/illegitimate, good/bad . . . followed by a 'mediation' of the paired categories thus distinguished."[3] In other words, in a mythical story, an opposition between two terms that cannot be reconciled (binary opposition), will be represented by two fictional surrogates, and these replacements will allow a reconciliation or mediation which the original pair could not receive. It is also evident that these opposite terms are usually very profound and fundamentally important ones.

2. Lévi-Strauss, *Structural Anthropology*, 226.
3. Leach, *Genesis as Myth and Other Essays*, 11.

The Function of Myth

The American anthropologists Elli Köngäs Maranda and Pierre Maranda have applied Lévi-Strauss's structural formula for myth to other types of folklore, and their results cast some significant light on the whole process under study in this chapter. They accept Lévi-Strauss's basis thesis that myth performs the specific task of mediating irreducible opposites. When they extend this formula to other genres of folklore, they arrive at a set of models that can be represented by a tree structure and that can also serve as a decision model for the storyteller (see figure 1).[4] The model in the figure obviously proceeds by a binary opposition at each step. If one chooses the negative (upper) option, the sequence and the story abort. If one chooses the positive (lower) option, one can then proceed to the next possibility. An example: (1) Contrast (or contradiction) is present between a certain peace-loving nation which possesses a huge supply of weapons. (2) Attempt to mediate by invoking fear of attack by another equally powerful nation. (3) Success in mediation as the nation's own people accept the story and the other nation gets nervous and bellicose. (4) Gain by mediation for munitions industry at home and for imperialist adventures abroad.

It is the introduction of the term "gain" in the diagram which will be the focus of our present concern. Think, for example, of the mythical or folklore story in which the hero starts out to solve the poverty-stricken situation of himself and his family. But instead of concluding in comfortable, middle-class suburbia, he ends up marrying the king's daughter, becoming heir to the throne, and moving

4. Maranda and Maranda, "Structural Models in Folklore," 26.

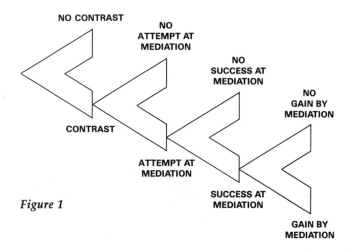

NO CONTRAST

NO ATTEMPT AT MEDIATION

NO SUCCESS AT MEDIATION

NO GAIN BY MEDIATION

CONTRAST

Figure 1

ATTEMPT AT MEDIATION

SUCCESS AT MEDIATION

GAIN BY MEDIATION

his family into the palace. That, I suppose, is "gain" (rags to great riches) and not just "mediation" (rags to clothes). Or, as the Marandas note, this last model of story "doubtless prevails in European folklore and probably also in other optimistic, 'winning,' and rich societies. There, lowly heroes start from poor conditions of life and rise, in a 'capitalistic' way, to positions of wealth and high social status. In this respect, the conception of after-life is much greedier in European than in Eskimo folklore: in the latter, adequate means of subsistence are enough to bring happiness."[5]

But the question of gain is even more fundamental and reaches from the social to the metaphysical or ontological level of human experience. When one looks back at myth from this vantage point, one notices that the whole process of mediation and reconciliation implies in itself a gigantic gain. Whether mediation is successful or not, or even gainful or not, one is establishing in, by, and through myth the conviction that mediation is possible. This is the

5. Maranda and Maranda, "Structural Models in Folklore," 136.

heart of myth, and it is also the profound and ontological "gain" therein. Here is myth at its most basic functional purpose. What myth does is not just to attempt the mediation in story of what is sensed as irreconcilable, but in, by, and through this attempt it establishes the possibility of reconciliation. No one, I suppose, has articulated better this function of myth than Pierre Maranda himself in a description which reflects both the difficulty and the poetry of mythical language:

> Myth . . . is the expression of the dynamic disequilibrium which is the (acknowledged) powerlessness to build adequate homomorphisms between incompatible and hence disturbing facts. It is the expression of the reluctant acknowledgement that the event is mightier than the structure. But myth is also and more than anything else the hallucinogenic chant in which mankind harmonizes the vagaries of history—the chant hummed for generations in the minds of men and humming itself in the human mind (that innate dream to reduce continuous randomness to a final pattern) as hinted at by Plato and Jung or, better, as amplified by Chomsky and Lévi-Strauss.[6]

It is much more important to believe in the possibility of solution than ever to find one in actuality. The gain or advantage of myth, and its basic function, is to establish that possibility itself.

Parable as Contradiction

In the process of discussing myth and the extension of Lévi-Strauss's mythical formula to other folklore genres by the Marandas, we found ourselves repeatedly thinking

6. Pierre Maranda, *Mythologies*, 213.

in terms of binary or paired opposition. Whether the mind must always so think or just tends to think that way much of the time, can be left aside for the moment. If we are thinking in binary opposites, however, one question is immediately obvious. Is there another kind of story, the binary opposite of myth, which does not create reconciliation for irreconcilables but which creates irreconciliation where before there was reconciliation? In other words, if we go back to the tree diagram in figure 1, must there not be a second bifurcation in that initial branch, as suggested in figure 2, (with my additions in italics)? It is the basic thesis of this book that a parable is a story which is the polar, or binary, opposite of myth. Parable brings not peace but the sword, and parable casts fire upon the earth which receives it.

In this diagram I have added a new branch to the "no contrast" branch of figure 1. Again, there is a binary opposition: "contrast not created/contrast created." If a storyteller chooses the former option, the story aborts immediately. If one opts for "contrast created," a parable is the result. But to stay in parable one must stop right there. If the storyteller starts to mediate the newly created contrast, the story starts slipping into the other main stem of the diagram and going back into myth.

I will use this understanding of parable within the possibilities of story both to establish a tradition of parable and to see if any or all of Jesus' stories are within this tradition. In parable, of course, we are not outside of story, which is to be outside humanity, but we are in story at the point where it shows awareness of its own inevitability and also its own relativity. Parable shows us the seams and edges of myth. Or, to recall an earlier image, it places us on the edge of the raft. It was to these two binary opposites within story that the literary critic Frank Ker-

Figure 2

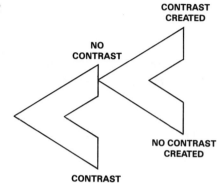

mode referred with the statement, "Myths are the agents of stability, fictions the agents of change."[7] Parables are fictions, not myths; they are meant to change, not reassure us.

Parable is always a somewhat unnerving experience. You can usually recognize a parable because your immediate reaction will be self-contradictory: "I don't know what you mean by that story but I'm certain I don't like it." To be human and to remain open to transcendental experience demands a willingness to be "parabled," or, as W. H. Auden suggests in "For the Time Being":

> Therefore, see without looking, hear without listening, breathe without asking:
> The Inevitable is what will seem to happen to you purely by chance;
> The Real is what will strike you as really absurd:
> Unless you are certain you are dreaming, it is certainly a dream of your own;
> Unless you exclaim—"There must be some mistake"
> —you must be mistaken.[8]

7. Kermode, *The Sense of an Ending*, 39.

39

Myth has a double function: the reconciliation of an individual contradiction and, more important, the creation of belief in the permanent possibility of reconciliation. Parable also has a double function which opposes that double function of myth. The surface function of parable is to create contradiction within a given situation of complacent security but, even more unnervingly, to challenge the fundamental principle of reconciliation by making us aware of the fact that we made up the reconciliation. Reconciliation is no more fundamental a principle than irreconciliation. You have built a lovely home, myth assures us; but, whispers parable, you are right above an earthquake fault.

In all of this I am not at all interested in elevating the adolescent pout to the level of transcendental experience. What matters to me in this discussion of parable is what L. M. Vail wrote in describing the philosophy of Martin Heidegger: "In the openness of authentic disclosure we admit the possibility of something unknown, even contradictory, to our world; for we *put into question* our own faculties—for instance, reason, will, the senses—rather than blindly measuring and evaluating what is real on the basis of these."[9] It is because I believe that there is only story and that parable is story grown self-conscious and self-critical that I wish to discuss parable in such detail in this book.

Between Myth and Parable

I have argued for myth and parable as the binary or polar opposites of story and have pointed to the philo-

8. Auden, in *Collected Longer Poems*, 138.
9. Vail, *Heidegger and Ontological Difference*, 64.

sophical implications of this polarity. Even though the rest of this work will concern itself exclusively with parable, it will be necessary to sketch certain other possibilities of story within these twin poles. In doing this I shall be following very closely the analysis of Sheldon Sacks in his book *Fiction and the Shape of Belief*.

Sacks sums up his purpose and his thesis as follows: "In pursuing the enquiry into the relationship between a novelist's moral beliefs, opinions, and prejudices and the work he creates, I have advanced the theory that all relevant works of prose fiction are organized according to one of three mutually exclusive types: satire, apologue, or action."[10] Sacks uses these three types for a critical analysis of the writings of certain eighteenth-century prose writers, especially Henry Fielding. First, satire: "A satire is a work organized so that it ridicules objects external to the fictional world created in it." The objects ridiculed may be "particular men, the institutions of men, traits presumed to be in all men, or any combination of the three." Second, apologue: "An apologue is a work organized as a fictional example of the truth of a formulable statement or a series of such statements." The informing principle that holds these two types of writing together as coherent wholes is that all the parts must contribute either to establishing ridicule in satire or in persuading the truth of the statements in apologue. Third, represented action: "An action is a work organized so that it introduces characters, about whose fates we are made to care, in unstable relationships which are then further complicated until the complication is finally resolved by the removal of the represented instability."[11] Most ordinary novels are actions as defined here.

10. Sacks, *Fiction and the Shape of Belief*, 7.
11. Sacks, *Fiction and the Shape of Belief*, 24–25.

41

This threefold schema of prose writing suggested by Sacks can be integrated within the schema of myth and parable as indicated in figure 3. This gives us a full spectrum of *story* and the distinctions between its parts can best be explained by the relationship of each to *world*. It is these relationships, in other words, which establish the different kinds of story, the different ways in story. But these relationships are not to world outside story, world which story describes and imitates, but to world inside story, world which story creates and defines.

This basic fivefold typology can be summarized like this: Myth establishes world. Apologue defends world. Action investigates world. Satire attacks world. Parable subverts world. It is clear, I hope, that parable can only subvert the world created in and by myth. There is no other world it can touch. It is possible to live in myth and without parable. But it is not possible to live in parable alone. To live in parable means to dwell in the tension of myth and parable. It is obvious, of course, that one can change from one myth (for example, capitalism) to another (for example, communism), and that every myth can have an antimyth. But a parable is not an antimyth, and it must be carefully distinguished from such. It is a story deliberately calculated to show the limitations of myth, to shatter world so that its relativity becomes apparent. It does not, as parable, replace one myth with another. Like

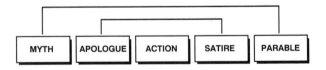

Figure 3

satire, parable keeps us humble by reminding us of limit. Like satire, parable is intrinsically negative. It is in fact the dark night of story, but precisely therein and thereby can it prepare us for the experience of transcendence. To borrow from "The Dry Salvages" of T. S. Eliot, you could say that parable is

> The backward look behind the assurance
> Of recorded history, the backward half-look
> Over the shoulder, towards the primitive terror.[12]

The best way I can think of to exemplify these five modes of story in a unified way is to take up the comic pages, say, of the *Chicago Tribune* and illustrate all five types of story from among the comic strips. Myth is represented by "Rick O'Shay," which continues the venerable Western myth of the virtuous gunslinger whose gun is fastest because his heart is purest. Apologue is rather blatant in "Dick Tracy," where law-and-order is advocated by such immortal sayings as, "Yes, *inevitably* a criminal's mind cracks first, then with reason perverted he fashions his own finish." You can usually see the apologue ("message") coming because Tracy, or whoever, will announce it, looking straight out of the strip at the reader. Action is found in the adventures of "Brenda Starr." We are made to care about Brenda through the course of interminable episodes because there is a basic "instability of relationship" introduced in the story by the fact that her boyfriend is always off in the jungle trying to stay alive on black orchid serum ("Home from the airport, Brenda falls on her bed in a flood of tears"). Satire is now very ably represented by "Doonesbury," with, for example, Mrs. Richardson asking her husband, "Elliot, don't you think it's about

12. Eliot, *Four Quartets*, 39.

TYPES OF STORY	RELATIONSHIP TO WORLD	CARTOON EXAMPLES
MYTH	establishes world	Rick O'Shay
APOLOGUE	defends world	Dick Tracy
ACTION	investigates world	Brenda Starr
SATIRE	attacks world	Doonesbury
PARABLE	subverts world	Basil

Figure 4

time you started looking for a job?" Parable is present, at times, in the recently arrived "Basil." Quite often this strip moves between whimsy and fantasy, but just as often there is a strong element of parable asking us why things might not be just as well some other way rather than the way we expected and presumed.[13]

Figure 4 brings together the five modes of story, their fivefold relationship to the world created in and by story, and these five examples.

This book is mostly about parable, which has been approached through its opposite, myth. The importance of

13. Those examples are taken from a random offering of the *Chicago Tribune* on the day I was writing this section. Very soon after its arrival, the story "Basil" ceased appearing. I phoned the editor to ask why, although I was suspicious that it was much too irreverent for survival. He said that it was unsuitable for their readership but bridled at the suggestion that it might have been censored because of reader disapproval.

the rest of the fivefold typology will appear later. I will try to show in the last chapter that Jesus' stories are parables as parables have been defined here, not historical allegories and moral example-stories, which is how the traditional interpretation has presented them. These latter would be forms of apologue, either defending how God acts or defining how we should act, and would be, in the above figure, almost as far from parable as one could go. They would be well on their way towards the polar opposite of what they were originally, well on their way to myth. This change would represent, for example, a far greater shift than that undergone by Jonathan Swift's satire *Gulliver's Travels*, which came to be read as an action, intended mainly for children.

3

The
Tradition
of Parable

I have suggested that parable is necessary, logically, as the binary opposite of myth. Myth proposes, parable disposes. Here I will try to establish that parable does exist and has a long and rich tradition of its own.

Structure and Development

Since it is impossible to compress a whole tradition in a few pages, I will examine only two stages in the development of parable as a literary genre, the earliest and the most recent stages. This will give some sense of the evolution of the parabolic form and will serve as an introduction to the tradition of parable itself. The first stage will be illustrated from two books of the Hebrew Bible and the final stage will be exemplified in the work of two modern novelists.

The difficulty in this approach will be to find some common ground on which to base comparisons of such disparate works of literature used as examples: the biblical books of Ruth and Jonah and the writings of Kafka and Borges. As in the previous chapter, structuralist analysis will be of prime importance in solving the problem.

The French structuralist critic Algirdas Julien Greimas has drawn attention to the fact that many folktales have a basic structure which could be outlined as in figure 5.[1]

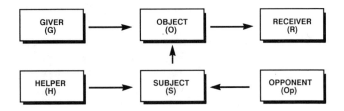

Figure 5

This can be very easily exemplified from any standard story in the private detective genre. The Giver is, for example, the insurance company which hires the detective to recover some lost and insured merchandise. The Object is this latter merchandise. The Receiver is the owner of the insured and stolen goods. The Subject is, of course, the private detective himself. The Opponent is whoever stole the merchandise. The Helper could be some Watson-like friend. This can be outlined as in figure 6. The variations that can be worked out for this pattern by combining in one person the Recipient and the Thief, and so on, are quite extensive.

Roland Barthes, another structuralist literary critic, has noted that there are actually three separate lines or axes, involved in Greimas' schematic structure. He called the

1. Greimas, *Sémantique structurale*, 180.

Giver-Object-Receiver (GOR) an axis of communication; the Subject-Object (SO) axis, one of volition, search, or quest; and the Helper-Subject-Opponent (HSOp) line an axis of test, trial, or ordeal.[2] This means that apart from stories like those just mentioned, in which all three axes and their six actants are present, there could also be stories in which only one, or only two, axes are involved. There could be stories, for example, using only the GOR axis of communication or the SO axis of search, or either of these with the HSOp axis of test. Second, he said that in many instances the tension of the story would actually consist in a "duel of persons." This means that one could have stories whose major action was not just the interplay of the six actants suggested by Greimas but, for example, a duel between two equal Subjects for the same Object (a love

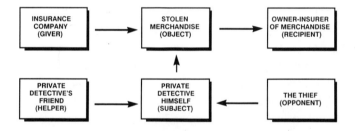

Figure 6

triangle) or even a duel between two equal Givers or two equal Receivers.

It is these two suggestions of Barthes that I shall use in offering a structural pattern which can be seen in parables at the two stages of their development to be investigated. A "duel of persons" on the axis of communication (GOR)

---

2. Barthes, "Introduction à l'analyse structurale des récits," 17.

will suffice to show the structural similarities between ancient and modern parables. In all cases to be considered I shall be analyzing the story either in terms of one Giver, two Objects, and two Receivers; or in terms of two Givers, two Objects, and one Receiver. There will be either a duel of Givers or of Receivers in each case. These two structures are outlined in figure 7.

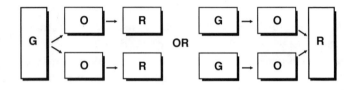

Figure 7

There is one final point. My argument will be that there is in every parabolic situation a battle of basic structures. There is the structure of expectation on the part of the hearer and there is the structure of expression on the part of the speaker. These structures are in diametrical opposition, and this opposition is the heart of the parabolic event. That is, the hearer expects that a certain Object (O+) will be given by a certain Giver (G+) to a certain Receiver (R+) and that the opposite Object (O−) may also be given by a certain other Giver (G−) to a certain opposite Receiver (R−). What actually happens in the parable is the reverse of what the hearer expects. The two possibilities are outlined in figure 8. If all these diagrams seem strange and abstract, please bear with me a while. I have not forgotten the warning of the poem "What Fifty Said" by Robert Frost, "I gave up fire for form till I was cold,"[3] or

3. Frost, *Poetry*, 267.

that of Auden's even more laconic admonition, "If speech can never become music, neither can it ever become algebra."[4] So now for application.

The Hebrew Bible

The first stage in the development of the parable form will be taken from the books of Ruth and Jonah in the Hebrew Bible. In the gospel of Luke (24:27) the Hebrew Bible is referred to by the phrase, "Moses and all the prophets." This twofold division reflects two of the great traditions of Israel, the legal and the prophetic. In Luke 24:44 this is expanded into "the law of Moses and the prophets and the psalms," so that a third major tradition, the sapiential or wisdom tradition, is added. My sugges-

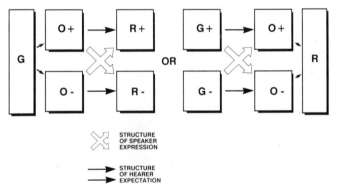

Figure 8

tion is that the books of Ruth and Jonah represent parables deliberately poised against the first two of these traditions, the legal and the prophetic. (For a parabolic attack on the

4. Auden, *The Dyer's Hand and Other Essays*, 24.

wisdom tradition's assurance that God rewards the good and punishes the wicked here on earth, read Ecclesiastes 2.) As parables, Ruth and Jonah do not intend to negate or destroy these magnificent traditions, but they do intend to remind Israel about the difference between the traditions of God and the God of the traditions.

The Book of Ruth

This book is really a short story and the synopsis given here should not be taken as a substitute for the four brief chapters of the story itself, which deserves to be read in its entirety.

Elimelech is a native of Bethlehem whom famine forces to migrate with his wife, Naomi, and their two sons into the non-Israelite regions of Moab. The father dies, the two sons marry, and eventually they also die. So, with five verses and three funerals, the stage is set for the story. Naomi decides to return home, and her daughters-in-law, Orpah and Ruth, want to accompany her. She manages to dissuade Orpah, but Ruth insists on returning with her. The words of her loyalty have justly become famous: "Entreat me not to leave you or to return from following you; for where you go I will go, and where you lodge I will lodge; your people shall be my people, and your God my God" (1:16). It is the time of the harvest and Ruth goes into the field of one Boaz to glean barley as the field is harvested. Boaz, a relative of the dead Elimelech, admires the loyalty of Ruth and makes certain that she is able to glean far more than her share. Naomi now takes over and tells Ruth to go to the threshing floor by night. There "when Boaz had eaten and drunk, and his heart was merry, he went to lie down at the end of the heap of grain. Then she came softly, and uncovered his feet, and lay down" (3:7). The story now moves to a climax. Boaz agrees to marry Ruth "in the morning" (3:13), but he must first get permission from another relative who has prior rights to both her land and her hand. This is swiftly done, and the story comes to a happy ending. "So Boaz took Ruth and she became his wife; and he went in to her, and the Lord gave her conception and she bore a son" (4:13).

If this beautiful story of fidelity and dignity had ended with the happiness of Naomi, it could be explained as an example of God's concern for and reward of the graciousness of Ruth herself. But the story actually ends with this genealogical statement: "They named him Obed; he was the father of David. Now these are the descendants of Perez; Perez was the father of Hezron, Hezron of Ram, Ram of Amminadab, Amminadab of Nashon, Nashon of Salmon, Salmon of Boaz, Boaz of Obed, Obed of Jesse, and Jesse of David" (4:17–22). In other words, it is twice repeated that Obed, the son of Ruth, was the grandfather of David, the great king of Israel.

Otto Eissfeldt has argued that "the Ruth narrative had originally nothing at all to do with David, but has only secondarily been made into a narrative concerning David's ancestors."[5] Why might this change have been made, so that the pastoral idyll now ends with the reiterated statement that Ruth of Moab was the great-grandmother of David? My suggested answer is that the book of Ruth is a parable, not an apologue or example story of the divine rewards for human fidelity.

To understand this biblical story as a parable, we need to look at the background against which it was written. The Babylonians had destroyed Jerusalem in 587 BCE and had deported large numbers of the most important and influential members of the population. The Babylonians

5. Eissfeldt, *The Old Testament: An Introduction*, 480.

fell before Cyrus and his Persians in 553, and in 538 Cyrus issued a decree allowing the exiles to return to Palestine. Under Persian tolerance, and despite tremendous internal and external difficulties, the returned exiles started to rebuild their shattered homeland under the guidance of Nehemiah and Ezra. It is easy to understand the intransigence that was needed to push through such a restoration to its completion. The walls of Jerusalem had to be rebuilt, the Temple and its worship restored, and, above all else, the Law of God, which was the very heart of the theocratic state, had to be reinstituted.

Ezra had the official mandate of the Persian imperial power to teach and enforce the Law of God. King Artaxerxes concluded his royal decree with these words: "Whoever will not obey the law of your God and the law of the king, let judgment be strictly executed upon him, whether for death or for banishment or for confiscation of his goods or his imprisonment" (Ezra 7:26). Ezra decided that such fidelity to God's Law not only forbade any intermarriage between Israelites and foreigners (it was a question of foreign wives, mainly) but also demanded the present and immediate divorce of all such marriages already contracted. Hence the confession and repentance of Ezra 10:2–3: "We have broken faith with our God and have married foreign women from the peoples of the land, but even now there is hope for Israel in spite of this. Therefore let us make a covenant with our God to put away all these wives and their children." There follows a great gathering where "all the people sat in the open square before the house of God, trembling because of this matter and because of the heavy rain" (10:9). (A little irony there, maybe?) The whole gathering agrees to divorce all foreign wives. "It is so; we must do as you have said. But the people are many, and it iṣ a time of heavy rain; we cannot stand in the open. Nor is this a work for one day or for two; for we have greatly transgressed in this matter" (10:12–13).

When the book of Ruth is read against this postexilic background of the divorce and abandonment of foreign wives and their children, the polemic of the genealogy becomes clear. Over against Ezra's decree of divorce, abandonment, and strict genealogical data stands this simple pastoral idyll. In Ezra 9:1–2 complaint is made to him that "the people of Israel" have gone to foreigners, among them "the Moabites," and "have taken some of their daughters to be wives for themselves and their sons." But the book of Ruth continually stresses that she is "a foreigner" (2:10), from Moab, and a Moabitess (1:1, 2, 4, 6, 7, 22; 2:2, 6, 21; 4:3, 5, 10). If Boaz had divorced Ruth and abandoned her child, Obed, what, then, of David? Or, in the diagram format of figure 9.

The Book of Jonah

Once again we are dealing with a short story that should be read in its entirety. John Miles has described this story as a parody "laughing at the Bible" itself.[6] John McKenzie has called it a "parable [whose] story seems to run directly counter to the ancient theology of election and covenant."[7] The book of Jonah places a parable not only against the entire prophetic tradition but against the very heart of the Bible itself. But, note well, against the Bible *within* the Bible. I shall summarize the story in four main points: the call, the mission, the message, and the anger of

5. Miles, "Laughing at the Bible," 168.
7. McKenzie, *A Theology of the Old Testament*, 121–22.

55

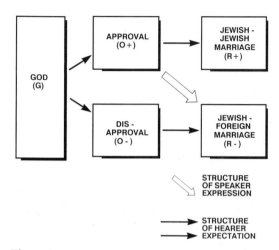

Figure 9

The hearer expects that God will grant approval to a
Jewish-Jewish marriage and disapproval to a Jewish-Foreign
one, but the story tells of divine approval to a Jewish-Foreign
union.

Jonah. In each of the drama's four acts what happens is
the exact opposite of what one expects in a story from the
prophetic tradition.

First, the call of Jonah: When the prophet Isaiah is called
to prophecy he is eager and willing for that high destiny.
In Isa 6:8–9: "I heard the voice of the Lord saying, 'Whom
shall I send, and who will go for us?' Then I said, 'Here am
I! Send me.' And he said, 'Go.'" When Jeremiah is called to
his vocation, he is at first afraid of its demands. In Jer 1:6
he responds, "Ah, Lord God! Behold, I do not know how to
speak, for I am only a youth." Whether diffident or
confident, however, the prophet must respond to his call
with obedience. This is the tradition. But what of Jonah's
call to prophecy? "Now the word of the Lord came to

56

Jonah the son of Amittai, saying, 'Arise, go to Nineveh, that great city, and cry against it; for their wickedness has come up before me.' But Jonah rose to flee to Tarshish from the presence of the Lord" (1:1–3). God commands him to go east by land. Jonah goes west by sea. A strange prophet, this.

Second, the mission: God succeeds in getting Jonah going in the right direction by having him thrown overboard in a storm, thrown, it should be noted, by pagan sailors who know enough to realize that one cannot "flee from the presence of the Lord" (1:10). Then comes the next indignity for the recalcitrant prophet. "And the Lord appointed a great fish to swallow up Jonah; and Jonah was in the belly of the fish three days and three nights" (1:17). And debate has raged for generations over what precise species of Mediterranean fish is large enough to swallow prophets without basic structural damage to them, all the while completely ignoring the delicious satire of the whole proceedings. This satire of the disobedient prophet continues with his ignominious arrival in the Persian Gulf: "And the Lord spoke to the fish, and it vomited out Jonah upon the dry land" (2:10).

Third, the message: God now starts all over again with Jonah. "Arise, go to Nineveh, that great city, and proclaim to it the message that I tell you" (3:2). When he arrives there and delivers his message, that "Yet forty days, and Nineveh shall be overthrown!" (3:4), the result is the most magnificent repentance in the whole history of the prophetic tradition. "And the people of Nineveh believed God; they proclaimed a fast, and put on sackcloth, from the greatest of them to the least of them" (3:5). Even the king: "he rose from his throne, removed his robe, and covered himself with sackcloth, and sat in ashes" (3:6). A supreme satiric thrust is still to come. The repentance extends even to the beasts. "Let neither man nor beast, herd nor flock, taste anything; let them not feed, or drink water, but let man and beast be covered with sackcloth, and let them cry mightily to God" (3:7–8).

Finally, the anger of Jonah, a concluding irony: God decides not to punish Nineveh after all. This gives Jonah a somewhat belated excuse for his initial refusal to obey the prophetic call. "I pray thee, Lord, is not this what I said when I was yet in my country? That is why I made haste to flee to Tarshish; for I knew that thou art a gracious God and merciful, slow to anger, and abounding in steadfast love, and repentest of evil." (4:2) So Jonah sits out in the desert, pouting, both because his prophecy of destruction has not come true (as if the purpose of prophecy was accuracy rather than repentance) and because the plant that has been shading him is withering. Then the final sentence, with God speaking: "And should I not pity Nineveh, that great city, in which there are more than a hundred and twenty thousand persons who do not know their right hand from their left, and also much cattle?" (4:11).

The structure of the parable is actually a double reversal of expectation rather than a single one, as in the book of Ruth. This reverse is outlined in figure 10 (compare with figure 9 above). It is also clear that, in this case, we have two Givers and one Receiver rather than the reverse situation as in the book of Ruth.

The city of Nineveh was the capital of the brutal Assyrian Empire. To see what biblical prophecy really thought of "that great city" one should read the book of Nahum, which gives an entire chapter to a gleeful detailing of its destruction. Nahum begins in 3:1: "Woe to that bloody city, all full of lies and booty—no end to the plunder." And he concludes his diatribe in 3:19: "There is no assuaging

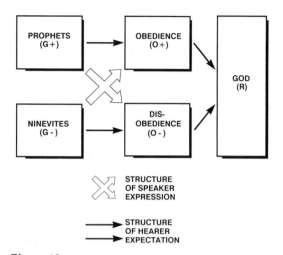

Figure 10

The hearer expects prophets to obey God, and pagans such as the Ninevites, especially, to disobey God. But the speaker tells a story in which a prophet disobeys and the Ninevites obey beyond all belief.

your hurt, your wound is grievous. All who hear the news of you clap their hands over you. For upon whom has not come your unceasing evil?" In the parabolic book of Jonah, there is, again, no destruction of the magnificent traditions of election, covenant, and prophecy. All that happens is what always happens in parable. God is given a little room in which to be God, and we are reminded of our finitude and our humanity. As Robert Frost has God explain to Job in his "A Masque of Reason,"

And it came out all right. I have no doubt
You realize by now the part you played
To stultify the Deuteronomist
And change the tenor of religious thought.

My thanks are to you for releasing me
From mortal bondage to the human race.
The only free will there at first was man's,
Who could do good or evil as he chose.
I had no choice but I must follow him
With forfeits and rewards he understood.[8]

The question posed by the books of Ruth and Jonah is this:
What if God does not play the game by our rules?

Some Modern Cases

The two modern authors I have chosen to indicate
contemporary developments in the parable form are the
Czech writer Franz Kafka and the Argentine author Jorge
Luis Borges. These two authors are chosen because their
stories are parables in the technical sense used in this
book.

In a special issue of the periodical *TriQuarterly* Ben Belitt
sums up the parabolic contributions of Kafka and Borges
with this comment: "as insights, parables serve what
might be called an epistemology of *loss*. Their value, as
knowledge, is to enhance our 'consciousness of ignor-
ance'—but that is the beginning of philosophy."[9] I suspect
it is also the start of religious experience.

Franz Kafka

Roland Barthes wrote this of Kafka in his collected
Critical Essays: "Kafka's technique says that the world's
meaning is unutterable, that the artist's only task is to
explore possible significations, each of which taken by
itself will be only a (necessary) lie but whose multiplicity

8. Frost, in *Poetry*, 475–76.
9. "The Enigmatic Predicament," 273.

60

will be the writer's truth itself."[10] This can serve as introduction to the parabolic nature of Kafka's work.

Kafka's short story, "Before the Law," which is excerpted from his novel *The Trial*, begins: "Before the Law stands a doorkeeper on guard. To this doorkeeper there comes a man from the country who begs for admittance to the Law. But the doorkeeper says that he cannot admit the man at the moment."[11] The man waits and waits, but the doorkeeper continues to refuse him admittance "yet." Finally, the man is dying, and he calls the doorkeeper over to his side. "'Everyone strives to attain the Law' . . . 'how does it come about, then, that in all these years no one has come seeking admittance but me?' The doorkeeper perceives that the man is at the end of his strength and that his hearing is failing, so he bellows in his ear: 'No one but you could gain admittance through this door, since this door was intended only for you. I am now going to shut it.'"[12]

One can recognize immediately the parabolic structure, with its single reversal, as shown in figure 11. After the story proper there is a discussion concerning it between K., the protagonist, and "the priest." Is the man at fault for not trying harder, or is the doorkeeper at fault for denying him admittance? At the very end the disturbing third alternative begins to loom before their eyes. Could it be that nobody is "at fault" for the situation except, of course, the Law which established such a situation. . . ?

There are certain standard reactions that I get from undergraduate college students when they read this story for the first time. Some find no problem in it since they read into it a Christian conclusion that presumes the man

10. Barthes, *Critical Essays*, 137.
11. Kafka, "Before the Law," 61.
12. Kafka, "Before the Law," 65.

61

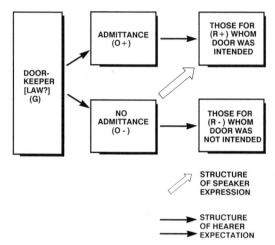

Figure 11

The hearer expects a doorkeeper to give admittance to those for whom the door was intended but no admittance to others. Instead, the story has no admittance given to a man for whom the door was specially planned.

is admitted *after* his death. To which I can only reply, as the priest does to K. in their discussion, "You have not enough respect for the written word and you are altering the story."[13] Most have a John Wayne reaction to the problem and blame the man for not forcing his way past the doorkeeper. This despite the story's clear warning that force would be futile: "But note that I am powerful. And I am only the lowest doorkeeper. From hall to hall keepers stand at every door, one more powerful than the other. Even the third of these has an aspect that even I cannot bear to look at."[14] Others blame the doorkeeper, even

13. Kafka, "Before the Law," 65.
14. Kafka, "Before the Law," 61.

though there is no indication in the story that he is exceeding his function and his responsibility. But there are always a few in every class who hear Kafka's challenge with all its disturbing clarity: what if life were like a door intended for you alone but through which you could not enter?

Jorge Luis Borges

The American novelist John Barth wrote an article on Borges for *The Atlantic Monthly* called "The Literature of Exhaustion." By this he meant the literature "of exhausted possibility." He discussed how a modern writer, precisely as modern, might have to make literature out of the experienced difficulty or even felt impossibility of making literature any longer. The novel is dead. Well, then, write a novel about the funeral. "Moreover, like all of Borges' work, it illustrates in other of its aspects my subject: how an artist may paradoxically turn the felt ultimacies of our time into material and means for his work—*paradoxically* because by doing so he transcends what had happened to be his refutation, in the same way that the mystic who transcends finitude is said to be enabled to live, spiritually and physically, in the finite world."[15] It is this which fascinates me with Borges and it is this which makes him a "parabler" in the sense used in this book.

Take, for example his short story "The Circular Ruins."[16] Because paraphrase fails dismally to convey the persuasive power of Borges' prose, I shall quote him often.

A stranger came ashore from the south by night and fell fainting amid the circular ruins of a "temple which was

15. Barth, "The Literature of Exhaustion," 32.
16. It can be found in at least four different collections of his work: *Ficciones, Labyrinths, A Personal Anthology,* and *The Aleph and Other Stories 1933–1969.* I cite it from that last collection.

destroyed ages ago by flames, which the swampy wilderness later desecrated, and whose god no longer receives the reverence of men." The stranger rested and slept. We are told that "his guiding purpose, though it was supernatural, was not impossible. He wanted to dream a man; he wanted to dream him down to the last detail and project him into the world of reality." He began by dreaming the circular ruins into a university lecture theater and listened carefully to the responses of the crowds of students who answer his questions. "He was in search of a soul worthy of taking a place in the world."

He dreamt day and night save for an hour or two at dawn. After ten days he had divided the students into passive recipients and active questioners "who from time to time hazarded reasonable doubts about what he taught." Finally, he chose one of these latter students, and dismissed all the rest. He concentrated totally on this one student. Then, catastrophe. He awoke to insomnia. He tried everything to resume dreaming but to no avail, and "in his almost endless wakefulness, tears of anger stung his old eyes." Only when he finally gave up trying to dream for a whole month did he finally fall asleep and was able to start all over again.

This time his first dream was of a human heart, and from there, in a period of one year, he built up, dream by dream, a full human being, although "the countless strands of hair were perhaps the hardest task of all." But the young man he had dreamed would not open his eyes. "Night after night, the man dreamed him asleep." Despondent, he almost destroyed the young man but, restraining himself, turned in his dream for aid from the god whose ruined temple he inhabited. This god revealed that its earthly name was Fire and that "through its magic the phantom of the man's dreams would be awakened to life in such a way that—except for Fire itself and the dreamer —every being in the world would accept him as a man of flesh and blood." Once the young man was alive, the god ordered him to be sent north to a second ruined temple to worship the god at his other shrine. "In the dreamer's dream, the dreamed one awoke."

Slowly the man inserted him, step by step, into reality. "On one occasion he commanded him to set up a flag on a distant peak. The next day, there on the peak, a fiery pennant shone." Finally, he sent the young man north and erased from his mind all memory of his apprenticeship.

Later, he worried about his "unreal son" when travelers from the north told him of a certain magician in a temple downstream who could walk unharmed on fire. "He feared that his son might wonder at this strange privilege and in some way discover his condition as a mere appearance."

This anxiety was interrupted by the arrival of a long drought which eventually precipitated a forest fire that threw the animals of the forest into a headlong panic. As had happened long before, the fire god's shrine was to be destroyed by fire. "For a moment, he thought of taking refuge in the river, but then he realized that death was coming to crown his years and to release him from his labors. He walked into the leaping pennants of flame. They did not bit into his flesh, but caressed him and flooded him without heat or burning. In relief, in humiliation, in terror, he understood that he, too, was an appearance, that someone else was dreaming him."

The story operates with a very subtle double reversal, as indicated in figure 12.

The reversal is developed in two steps. First, we see what we presume is an "ordinary" human being giving real existence to a dreamed figure, but, at the very end, we

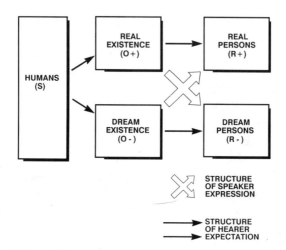

Figure 12

We expect human beings to give real existence only to real persons and to distinguish dream existence for dream persons, but the story reverses these expectations.

discover that this ordinary human being was himself dreamed into reality by somebody else. At that point real/dreamed merge and fluctuate, and we ask: Is everybody, then, dreamed of another?

This question may seem just a game of rhetorical whimsy unless we think of its ontological implications. We know that storytellers and dramatists "dream up" characters and that the best of these become both international and immortal. They are more real than real persons. I can call somebody a "Hamlet" and be understood across centuries and continents. If there is only story, as this book has argued, then we are all characters in vast interlayers of story. We are all dreamed up by both ourselves and by others. Is it not perfectly ordinary language to speak of living in the nightmare of Hitler's Europe? This tale of Borges is a parable against the claim of a fixed reality, an objective world out there waiting for our neutral perusal. The story reminds us of what Borges himself said elsewhere: "We must go even further; we must suspect that there is no universe in the organic, unifying sense inherent in that ambitious word."[17] There is only story, and that means there is only carefully disciplined dreaming.

I shall conclude with another quotation from Borges which might well have stood as the epigraph for this book. "This will be our destiny—to give ourselves to syntax, to its treacherous linkage, to imprecision, to perhaps, to the exaggerated emphasis, to buts, to the hemisphere of lies and shadows in our sayings."[18] In a word, to story.

The Art of the Parable

So much for arrows and diagrams, for systems and structures, and for what the poet Pablo Neruda calls one's "shipshape box of tricks."[19] Is that all there is to parables, a few lines and a few arrows? A parable is rather like a person. Everyone has to have a skeletal system, but we usually take its presence absolutely for granted unless a situation of structural damage arises. But it is not the skeletal system that renders persons interesting or attractive. The skeleton is there and surgeons know it. So also with parables. I have been analyzing only their skeletal systems. Now a few words about their beauty and their art.

How exactly can one tell a story which attacks and undermines the hearer's structure of expectation without

17. Borges, "The Analytical Language of John Wilkins," 104.
18. Cited in Barrenechea, *Borges the Labyrinth Maker*, 81.
19. Neruda, "Autumn Testament," in *Selected Poems*, 405.

the hearer simply shrugging off the attack by stating that one's parabolic story just could not happen? It is in the surface structure and texture that the parabler must use consummate skill so that the deep structure of the parable gets into the hearer's consciousness and is only felt in its full force there when it is too late to do much about it.

Two examples will have to suffice. In the Kafka story examined above we are persuaded to accept the story's "realistic" possibility because we see it unroll before our very eyes. We see the "doorkeeper in his furred robe, with his huge pointed nose and long, thin, Tartar beard,"[20] and we, like the man seeking admittance, "have learned to know even the fleas in the doorkeeper's collar."[21] How can we deny the actuality of such a doorkeeper when we have seen the very fleas in his collar? Or, as a second example, note the details in the Borges story. He opens it with what seems like an exact geographical designation. The stranger's "home was among the numberless villages upstream on the steep slopes of the mountain, where the Zend language is barely tainted with Greek and where lepers are rare."[22] We get out a map. But then we recall the interchange between Borges and a journalist concerning the title story of his collection *The Aleph and Other Stories 1933–1969*: "'Ah,' said the journalist, 'so the entire thing is your own invention. I thought it was true because you gave the name of the street.' I did not dare to tell him that the naming of streets is not much of a feat."[23]

It may even be conjectured that parable always has to be short, like all the examples cited above. Borges has admitted that he cannot write a novel and has suggested

20. Kafka, "Before the Law," 61.
21. Kafka, "Before the Law," 63.
22. Borges, "The Aleph," 34.
23. Borges, "The Aleph," 190.

that Kafka could not either, even though he tried it a few times.[24] Maybe, and I would leave it only as a maybe, parable has to be short just as myth tends to be long.

It is clear that parable is really a story event and not just a story. One can tell oneself stories but not parables. One cannot really do so just as one cannot really beat oneself at chess or fool oneself completely with a riddle one has just invented. It takes two to parable.

24. Burgin, *Conversations*, 60.

4

Jesus as Parabler

Up to this point I have talked only of spoken or written parables, of parables of word. Here I wish to begin with parables of deed, parables which are enacted rather than just spoken or written down. One can oppose a structure of expectation by word and also by deed.

Parable and Deed

Parabolic deeds are part of the recent experience of protest in this country. If a black minister sat at a segregated lunch counter or if a rabbi poured blood over draft files or if a priest burned his country's flag, the action forced the viewer to face the following structural dilemma as the minister of God's word was led off to jail, as in figure 13. The action begets a series of very disturbing questions, and such is, of course, the very precise purpose of the action. Bad: why are ministers in jail (single reversal)? Worse still: does this mean that criminals are not in jail (double reversal)? Worst: what of the government

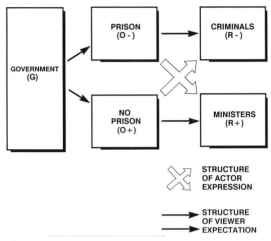

Figure 13

One expects the government to give prison to criminals but no prison to ministers. But if ministers go to prison, are the criminals free? And what then of the government...

which creates such an anomalous situation? And now to parabolic deed in the case of Jesus.

John R. Donahue wrote a very interesting article called "Tax Collectors and Sinners" in 1971. His general conclusions are significant for our present point. It is clear that stories concerning Jesus' fellowship with toll collectors and sinners belong to the earliest strata of the gospel tradition; even though these stories have certainly been changed and modified in transmission, they still contain historical reminiscences of the ministry of Jesus.[1] Who exactly were these people with whom Jesus is accused of consorting? In the classical publican system of taxation the

1. Donahue, "Tax Collectors and Sinners," see esp. 48–49, 54, 59–60.

ruler gave complete charge of all taxes to local leading
citizens who acted as tax-farmers, or publicans. These
persons would pay the ruler a set amount in advance, and
it would thereafter be their problem to get sufficient taxes
and profits back from the ordinary people. This system
was not in practice in Palestine in the New Testament
period. In the strict sense of the word, therefore, no real
"publicans" appear in the gospel texts. The direct taxes, at
that time, were under the supervision of the central authority; it was the indirect taxes, the tolls and other im-
posts, that were farmed out to individual lessees. This
farming of taxes brought with it all the evils of dishonesty
and exorbitant tariffs that could be expected from such a
system. We are dealing, then, with toll-collectors rather
than with publicans or even tax-collectors in the gospel
texts. This is why, for instance, we come across them at
those commercial centers when the collection of tolls
would be expected. We have Levi, the toll-collector, at
Capernaum, in Mark 2:14, and also Zacchaeus, the head
toll-collector, at Jericho, in Luke 19:2. Why "toll-collectors"
would be synonymous with "sinners" is clear from such
places as Luke 3:12, when John is baptizing. "Tax collectors
also came to be baptized, and said to him, 'Teacher, what
shall we do?' And he said to them, 'Collect no more than is
appointed you.'" In summary, then, the principal reason
for the scandal of Jesus would be his association with
dishonest people. The phrase "toll-collectors and sinners"
would not refer to two separate groups but to a single
group. It would mean "toll-collectors because they are
sinners."

What is striking in all this is that the earliest layers of the
gospel traditions record this scandalous association of
Jesus with such dishonest people, but they are not very
clear about its purpose. If these people all abandoned their

morally dangerous, if not downright dishonest, profession, why the scandal? There would hardly be room for criticism if Jesus' association with them obtained repentance, as in the story in Luke 19:7–8: "And when they saw it they all murmured, 'He has gone in to be the guest of a man who is a sinner.' And Zacchaeus stood and said to the Lord, 'Behold, Lord, the half of my goods I give to the poor; and if I have defrauded any one of anything, I restore it fourfold.'" I would suggest that the association was deliberately shocking and intentionally parabolic rather than a prelude to or a result of repentance. It was intended to raise questions of who was right and wrong before God and of how securely or self-righteously such decisions could be rendered. This shock can be outlined as in figure 14. The parabolic deed, precisely as parabolic, does not exalt the toll-collectors as virtuous. It is not a manifesto for theft. But it reminds everyone that God is even more important than ethics and that God may not always approve our moral judgments.

Parable and Humor

In the fivefold typology of story given above in figure 14, I noted how close parable is to satire. This section will focus on the satirical humor present in Jesus' parables, taking as examples the parables of the Mustard Seed and of the Lost Sheep and Lost Coin.

The Mustard Seed

The parable can be told from the text of Luke 13:18–19. "He said therefore, 'What is the kingdom of God like? And to what shall I compare it? It is like a grain of mustard seed which a man took and sowed in his garden; and it grew and became a tree, and the birds of the air made nests in its

74

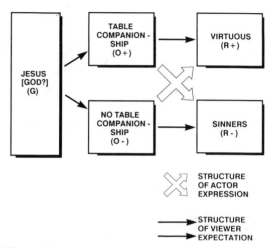

Figure 14

One expects Jesus as a prophet of God to consort with the
virtuous and not with sinners. If he does the opposite, does
this mean that the virtuous are sinners and sinners virtuous,
or what?

branches.'" The mustard seed was proverbial for its small
size. Recall the words of Jesus in Luke 17:6: "And the Lord
said, 'If you have faith as a grain of mustard seed, you
could say to this sycamine tree, "Be rooted up, and be
planted in the sea," and it would obey you.'" Jesus asso-
ciates the kingdom of God with this mustard plant, and
the text concludes with the pictorial image of birds nesting
in its branches.

This image reminds one of another somewhat similar
image in the Hebrew Bible.[2] In Ezek 31:2–6 the prophet is
told by God,

2. The italics in the following passages are mine.

Say to Pharaoh of Egypt and to his multitude: *'Whom are you like* in your greatness? Behold *I will liken you to* a cedar in Lebanon, with fair branches and forest shade, and of great height, its top among the clouds. The waters nourished it, the deep made it *grow* tall, making its rivers flow round the place of its planting, sending forth its streams to all the trees of the forest. So it towered high above all the trees of the forest; its boughs *grew* large and its branches long, from abundant water in its shoots. All the *birds of the air made their nests in its boughs.*

The power of the Egyptian empire is like that of Lebanon's mighty cedar, with all the other nations under its branches. Exactly the same figure is used for Nebuchadnezzar, head of the Babylonian empire, in Dan 4:10–12: "I saw, and behold, a tree in the midst of the earth; and its height was great. The tree *grew* and became strong, and its top reached to heaven, and it was visible to the end of the whole earth. Its leaves were fair and its fruit abundant, and in it was food for all. The beasts of the field found shade under it, and the *birds of the air dwelt in its branches.*" Again, a great and mighty tree with birds in its branches is a symbol of imperial power and majesty. Finally, in Ezek 17:22–23 the Lebanese cedar is again used but this time to image the Messiah himself as a cedar shoot whence would grow the messianic kingdom. "Thus says the Lord God: 'I myself will take a sprig from the lofty top of the cedar, and will set it out; I will break off from the topmost of its young twigs a tender one, and I myself will plant it upon a high and lofty mountain; on the mountain height of Israel will I plant it; that it may bring forth boughs and bear fruit; and become a noble cedar; and under it will dwell all kinds of beasts; in the shade of its branches *birds of every sort will nest.*'"

So, in the biblical traditions before Jesus, the great cedar of Lebanon, with birds in its branches, was considered a fitting image for the mighty imperial kingdoms of Meso-potamia and Egypt, and even for the Messiah and the messianic kingdom itself. But, against such a tradition, Jesus chooses a far more humble image, one which is a deliberate lampoon on the cedar's pretentiousness. The kingdom of God is not like the proverbial cedar of Leba-non but is like the very ordinary mustard plant. This is a satiric thrust at the earlier image with its apocalyptic tree whose "top reached to heaven" in Dan 4:11, the tree with its "top among the clouds" in Ezek 31:3. This ironic pur-pose explains certain features of Luke's text. The tradition does not seem to have appreciated the irony of Jesus' story. So it tried to bring Jesus' story more into line with the earlier tradition by calling the mustard shrub a "tree" and by having the birds "nest" in its branches. In the original story they would have been on the ground seek-ing the seed in the shade of the tree. By doing this, of course, they would only have highlighted the incompati-bility of mustard "tree" and cedar of Lebanon! One must presume that the tradition was not quite as much at home with this gentle satire on the messianic cedar as Jesus obviously was. Possibly it should have reread Ezek 17:24: "And all the trees of the field shall know that I the Lord bring low the high tree, and make high the low tree, dry up the green tree, and make the dry tree flourish." And trees shall be shrubs, and shrubs trees.

The Lost Sheep and the Lost Coin

The two stories appear in tandem format in Luke 15:1–10. [1]

Now the tax collectors and sinners were all drawing near to hear him. [2] And the Pharisees and the scribes murmured, saying, 'This man receives sinners and eats with them.' ³So he told them this parable: ⁴'What man of you, having a hundred sheep, if he has lost one of them, does not leave the ninety-nine in the wilderness, and go after the one which is lost, until he finds it? ⁵And when he has found it, he lays it on his shoulders, rejoicing. ⁶And when he comes home, he calls together his friends and his neighbors, saying to them, "Rejoice with me, for I have found my sheep which was lost." ⁷Just so, I tell you, there will be more joy in heaven over one sinner who repents than over ninety-nine righteous persons who need no repentance. ⁸Or what woman, having ten silver coins, if she loses one coin, does not light a lamp and sweep the house and seek diligently until she finds it? ⁹And when she has found it, she calls together her friends and neighbors, saying, "Rejoice with me, for I have found the coin which I had lost." ¹⁰Just so, I tell you, there is joy before the angels of God over one sinner who repents.

When the twin stories are read within their present interpretive frames, as given in Luke 15:1–3, 7, 10, there are no problems concerning their meaning, as outlined in figure 15. In the present Lukan context, in other words, Jesus is the one who searches, and sinners are those for whom he searches. But here is an interesting point. In John 10 this image is expanded to a full discussion of Jesus as the Good Shepherd who "calls his own sheep by name and leads them out. When he has brought out all his own, he goes before them, and the sheep follow him for they know his voice" (10:3–4). Not only does Jesus the shepherd lead his flock to water and to pasture but he even dies to protect them. "I am the good shepherd. The good shep-

	LUKE 15:3-7	LUKE 15:8-10
JESUS =	The Shepherd	The Housewife
TAX COLLECTORS AND SINNERS =	The Lost Sheep	The Lost Coin
ANGELS OF GOD IN HEAVEN =	Friends and Neighbors	Friends and Neighbors

Figure 15

herd lays down his life for his sheep. He who is a hireling and not a shepherd, whose own the sheep are not, sees the wolf coming and leaves the sheep and flees; and the wolf snatches them and scatters them. He flees because he is a hireling and cares nothing for the sheep. I am the good shepherd" (10:11–14). But nobody in the entire New Testament literature picked up the second and parallel story in Luke and developed the image of Jesus as the Good Housewife. If Jesus and/or God could be the Good Shepherd of the first story in Luke 15:3–7, why not also the Good Housewife of Luke 15:8–10? Is this, then, the ironic humor of these twin stories? Is one trapped into having God and/or Jesus, if a Good Shepherd (male), then also a Good Housewife (female)? Or is there an even more profound level of irony hidden in the two stories?

Modern biblical scholarship has taught us to distinguish between the stories of Jesus in their original intentionality and in their present interpretations within the gospel texts. We shall see more on this possible difference between original function and final evangelical usage in the next section. I am going to leave aside for the moment the interpretive frames in Luke 15:1–3, which give a "setting" for the parables, and also the concluding application for each one in 15:7 and in 15:10. For now I want to look at the two isolated stories as read in 15:4–6 and 15:8–9. Both tell of a loss, a successful search, and of the great rejoicing at a happy outcome to the initial problem.

There are two other parables of Jesus which are very similar to this sequence. These are also given in tandem format in Matt 13:44–46. They are the parables of the Hidden Treasure and the Pearl. "The kingdom of heaven is like treasure hidden in a field, which a man found and covered up; then in his joy he goes and sells all that he has and buys that field. Again, the kingdom of heaven is like a merchant in search of fine pearls, who, on finding one pearl of great value, went and sold all that he had and bought it." In these parables the searcher is usually seen as the human person and the object found is God or the kingdom of God (or of heaven). I would suggest that this is also what Jesus, as distinct from Luke, intended the stories of the Lost Sheep and the Lost Coin to indicate as well. In the original stories of Jesus *we* are the searchers, shepherd and housewife, male and female, and that for which we search is the kingdom of God whose finding is the occasion for communal rejoicing. Hence the "joy" of Matt 13:44 is exactly the same as the "joy" of Luke 15:6 and 9.

If this interpretation is correct, the irony is immediately evident. Israel had a long and magnificent tradition of God as the shepherd of his people. Recall, for example, these prophetic texts: In Isa 40:10–11, "Behold, the Lord God comes with might, and his arm rules for him. . . . He will feed his flock like a shepherd, he will gather the lambs in his arms, he will carry them in his bosom, and gently lead those that are with young." Since the leaders of his people have proved themselves false shepherds, God himself must find new shepherds. So Jer 23:1–4:

"Woe to the shepherds who destroy and scatter the sheep of my pasture!" says the Lord. Therefore thus says the Lord, the God of Israel, concerning the shepherds who care for my people: "You have scattered my flock, and have driven them away, and you have not attended to them. Behold, I will attend to you for your evil doings," says the Lord. "Then will I gather the remnant of my flock out of all the countries where I have driven them, and I will bring them back to their fold, and they shall be fruitful and multiply. I will set shepherds over them who will care for them, and they shall fear no more, nor be dismayed, neither shall any be missing," says the Lord.

Indeed, since human shepherds have failed God's flock so badly, God himself will have to be their shepherd. This is the theme of the entire chapter of Ezekiel 34, and is expressed climactically in 34:11–12: "For thus says the Lord God: Behold, I, I myself will search for my sheep, and will seek them out. As a shepherd seeks out his flock when some of his sheep have been scattered abroad, so will I seek out my sheep; and I will rescue them from all places where they have been scattered on a day of clouds and thick darkness."

Once again, Jesus' story appears as a gentle and ironic reversal of this great tradition. For the prophets, God was the shepherd and the searcher, and his people were the lost and wandering sheep, the object of God's search. For Jesus, it is the opposite. We are the searchers, but we search for what we have lost, for what was ours "in the beginning." In ironic humor Jesus makes God the lost sheep and the lost coin, and all of us, male and female alike, searchers for what we have lost. So Jesus called *us*, long ago, *the Shepherd of God*.

Parable and Word

In this section I will examine a few of the parables expressed by Jesus in word rather than in deed.

The Pharisee and the Publican

Here is the story as told in Luke 18:10–13, leaving aside the opening and closing frames of 18:9 and 18:14: "Two men went up into the temple to pray, one a Pharisee and the other a tax collector. The Pharisee stood and prayed thus with himself, 'God, I thank thee that I am not like other men, extortioners, unjust, adulterers, or even like this tax collector. I fast twice a week, I give tithes of all that I get.' But the tax collector, standing far off, would not even lift up his eyes to heaven, but beat his breast, saying, 'God, be merciful to me a sinner!'" A closing remark makes sure the reader doesn't miss the reversal: "I tell you this man went down to his house justified rather than the other."

There is an immediate problem. Parables are supposed to overturn one's structure of expectation and therein and thereby to threaten the security of one's established world. Such terms as "Pharisee" and "Publican" (or toll collector) evoke no immediate visceral reaction or expectation from a modern reader. In fact, after centuries of extremely nasty and quite inaccurate polemics against the Pharisees by Christians, the former have become almost stereotyped villains rather than the revered moral leaders they were at the time of Jesus. So, our structure of expectation is not that of the original hearers of the parable, and the parable now leaves us emotionally rather cold. No doubt we can have it all explained to us in terms of its original historical

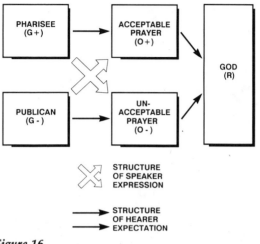

Figure 16

The hearer expects the Pharisee's prayer to be accepted by God and the Publican's to be rejected, but the story has the opposite happen.

impact within the language possibilities of Jesus' own day and audience. But a parable which has to be explained is, like a joke in similar circumstances, a parable which has been ruined *as parable*. The structure can be outlined as in figure 16.

Two items of folklore information may serve to underline the unexpectedness of Jesus' juxtaposition of the virtuous Pharisee and the dishonest Publican.

Heddy Jason wrote an interesting doctoral dissertation about sacred tales collected from Mediterranean and Near Eastern Jews who lived in Muslim countries for at least part of their past.[3] With the establishment of the state of Israel this society ceased to exist for the most part, its

3. Jason, *Conflict and Resolution*.

members gradually emigrating to Israel. She has this conclusion about the stories:

> The religious leader is implicitly the representative of the supreme values of the society and a questioning of his personal qualities or his right to leadership detracts from the validity of these values. For this reason there is not a single story in the whole Jewish Near Eastern material at our disposal which portrays the rabbi in a negative light or ridicules him as, on the contrary, the priest is frequently ridiculed in the Christian-European tradition, or as, occasionally, is the rabbi in Jewish European society.[4]

We today have to exercise some imagination to appreciate the shock of such a devastatingly simple reversal as that given in Jesus' short parable.

A second example shows that Jesus' story is not only unusual in his own tradition, but also quite unexpected against the general background of folktales themselves. In W. R. Bascom's "Folklore and Anthropology," he says, "In addition to the obvious function of entertainment or amusement, folklore serves to sanction the established beliefs, attitudes, and institutions, both sacred and secular, and it plays a vital role in education in nonliterate societies."[5] In another essay, he asks the rhetorical question, "There is no difficulty, of course, in finding instances in folklore where laziness, complacency, or the lack of ambition and initiative are condemned, but are there any which suggest that the individual destroy or even disregard the institutions and conventions of his society?"[6] It is precisely this that Jesus' parable suggests.

4. Jason, *Conflict and Resolution,* 1.
5. Dundes, *Study of Folklore,* 33.
6. Dundes, *Study of Folklore,* 297.

The Good Samaritan

This is possibly the best known of Jesus' stories. It was this story which initiated my own interest in parable several years ago. It occurred to me then, and I have not been able to exhaust this subject in my own mind as yet, that there seemed to be a totally different, even generically different, meaning to this story at an earlier level than is now given to it within the interpretive frames of Luke 10:25–29 and 10:36.

The present frames in Luke 10 make this story an example of how one should help one's neighbor in distress and, indeed, even one's enemy, if in need of assistance. It is told in answer to the lawyer's question, "And who is my neighbor?" (10:29) As the answer to such a question, the story clearly means that one's neighbor is anyone in need, even an enemy. But, let us leave aside the editorial frames and see the story as story, in Luke 10:30–35:

> A man was going down from Jerusalem to Jericho, and he fell among robbers, who stripped him and beat him, and departed, leaving him half dead. Now by chance a priest was going down that road; and when he saw him he passed by on the other side. So likewise a Levite, when he came to the place and saw him, passed by on the other side. But a Samaritan, as he journeyed, came to where he was; and when he saw him, he had compassion, and went to him and bound up his wounds, pouring on oil and wine; then he set him on his own beast and brought him to an inn, and took care of him. And the next day he took out two denarii and gave them to the innkeeper, saying, "Take care of him and whatever more you spend, I will repay you when I come back."

As with the last story, there are terms in this narrative that have to be understood by a modern reader. The storyteller is a Jew talking to fellow Jews, possibly in a Jerusalem setting (from the oblique reference to the robbed man as going down from Jerusalem to Jericho). The traveler is "one of us," in a location we can all easily imagine, says the storyteller. Those who refuse aid are official religious leaders, a "priest" and a "Levite," chosen most likely because of the Jerusalem setting of the teller. This is the first surprise, but the second shock is even greater. The person who performs the good act and helps the wounded man is a Samaritan, a socio-religious outcast. As John 4:9 put it simply and summarily, "Jews have no dealings with Samaritans." That is the problem. The "good" act evilly and the "bad" act virtuously. But if the story really intended to encourage help to one's neighbor in distress or even to one's enemy in need, would it not have been much better to have a wounded Samaritan in that ditch and have a Jew stop to aid him?

Since "priest," "Levite," and "Samaritan" have no immediate emotional connotations for the modern reader, I would like to rephrase the story in contemporary dress and attempt to convey anew its shock and its challenge. First the story: The storyteller is a priest in a Roman Catholic pulpit in Belfast. The wounded man "lived on the Falls Road," that is, obliquely, he was one of us. A member of the I.R.A. passed him by. So did a Catholic nun. A Protestant terrorist stopped and helped him. Fill out the details. What is the reaction of the hearers? Second story: The storyteller has just returned from Vietnam at the time when American soldiers were still fighting there and is on the evening news. The wounded person is a woman correspondent for NBC. Those who pass by without helping her are, first, an American Green Beret and second, a

South Vietnamese soldier. She is saved, finally, by a guerilla fighting with the Viet Cong. Fill out the details. What viewer reactions will be mailed in to the station?

In each of these stories the teller would, of course, fill in the action of the helper in great detail. In fact more than half the length of the story should be given over to how the unexpected helper acts. My question is this: Do we really think that the two storytellers would be able to convince an audience which was about to lynch them that all they were trying to say was: Love your enemies? When I tried out the second story on a class of college freshmen I found that many could accept the possibility of assistance from the Vietcong (this was in 1973) but that they said, "you should have left out the part about the Green Beret." The students sensed immediately that something more than "help your neighbor" or even "help your enemy in distress" was going on in the Belfast and Vietnam stories. So, apart from the problem that the terms of the Good Samaritan story evoke no immediate emotional reactions from the contemporary reader, the structure is still clearly that of parable, as in figure 17. That is why, for those who like to count words in Greek, there are forty-six words given to what precedes the arrival of the Samaritan on the scene but sixty words devoted to his arrival and, step-by-step, to his reaction. Since this reaction is so unexpected, it must be spelled out in explicit detail. The hearer must not be able to shrug it off by saying: No Samaritan would act that way! He must feel instead: I have just seen the wine and the oil, the donkey, and the inn. I have just seen the two denarii exchange hands and I have just heard the Samaritan discuss the situation with the innkeeper. . . . But whether one's mind reacts properly or not, the Good Samaritan ("the good terrorist" today?) is an attack on the structure of expectation and not a story which inculcates

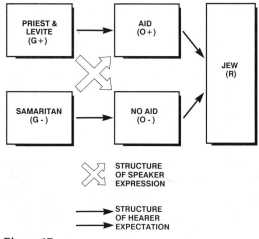

STRUCTURE
OF SPEAKER
EXPRESSION

STRUCTURE
OF HEARER
EXPECTATION

Figure 17

The hearer expects the Priest and Levite to help and the Samaritan to refuse assistance, but the story details exactly the opposite.

assistance to those in distress although, of course, it takes it absolutely for granted that assistance is required in such a case.

The Great Feast

The two previous parables were recorded only in Luke and the analysis was therefore fairly simple. The parable of the Great Feast is much more involved, and the investigation is in effect a miniature introduction to modern gospel criticism. The story appears in three different versions. The first two are in the canonical gospels in the New Testament, in Matthew 22:1–14 and Luke 14:16–24. The version in Matthew has two separate parts, the feast in 22:1–10 and the wedding garment in 22:11–14.

¹And again Jesus spoke to them in parables, saying,
²"The kingdom of heaven may be compared to a king
who gave a marriage feast for his son, ³and sent his
servants to call those who were invited to the marriage feast; but they would not come. ⁴Again he sent
other servants, saying, 'Tell those who are invited,
Behold, I have made ready my dinner, my oxen and
my fat calves are killed, and everything is ready; come
to the marriage feast.' ⁵But they made light of it and
went off, one to his farm, another to his business,
⁶while the rest seized his servants, treated them
shamefully, and killed them. ⁷The king was angry,
and he sent his troops and destroyed those murderers
and burned their city. ⁸Then he said to his servants,
'The wedding is ready, but those invited were not
worthy. ⁹Go therefore to the thoroughfares, and invite to the marriage feast as many as you find.' ¹⁰And
those servants went out into the streets and gathered
all whom they found, both bad and good; so the
wedding hall was filled with guests.

"¹¹But when the king came in to look at the guests,
he saw there a man who had no wedding garment;
¹²and he said to him, 'Friend, how did you get in here
without a wedding garment?' And he was speechless.
¹³Then the king said to the attendants, 'Bind him
hand and foot, and cast him into the outer darkness;
there men will weep and gnash their teeth: ¹⁴For
many are called but few are chosen.'"

The second account is in Luke 14:16–24, but note that in
this case there is only the feast story and nothing about
any wedding garment. ¹⁶

But he said to him, "A man once gave a great banquet,
and invited many; ¹⁷and at the time for the banquet

89

he sent his servant to say to those who had been invited, 'Come, for all is now ready.' [18] But they all alike began to make excuses. The first said to him, 'I have bought a field, and I must go out and see it; I pray you, have me excused.' [19] And another said, 'I have bought five yoke of oxen, and I go to examine them; I pray you, have me excused.' [20] And another said, 'I have married a wife, and therefore I cannot come.' [21] So the servant came and reported this to his master. Then the householder in anger said to his servant, 'Go out quickly to the streets and lanes of the city, and bring in the poor and maimed and blind and lame.' [22] And the servant said, 'Sir, what you commanded has been done, and still there is room.' [23] And the master said to the servant, 'Go out to the highways and hedges, and compel people to come in, that my house may be filled. [24] For I tell you, none of those men who were invited shall taste my banquet.'"

The third version needs a few words of explanation. Around the same time that those famous scrolls were discovered at Qumran on the northwestern shore of the Dead Sea, another collection of manuscripts was found at Nag Hammadi in Upper Egypt. These were written in Coptic and seem to be the remnants of a library belonging to a gnostic sect. One of the documents, The Gospel according to Thomas, is of special importance for the present discussion. This is not a gospel in the usual sense of that term. It does not have the standard "story" format, starting with John the Baptist and ending with Jesus' death and resurrection. Instead it has around 114 sayings and parables of Jesus, most of them beginning with a simple "Jesus said." What concerns us here is that we have another version of the parable of the Great Feast in this apocryphal, or noncanonical gospel, in its saying (or logion) 64. Here is that version:

> Jesus said: "A man had guest-friends, and when he had prepared the dinner, he sent his servants to invite the guest-friends. He went to the first, he said to him: 'My master invites thee.' He said, 'I have some claims against some merchants; they will come to me in the evening; I will go and give them my orders. I pray to be excused from the dinner.' He went to another, he said to him: 'My master has invited thee.' He said to him 'I have bought a house and they request me for a day. I will have no time.' He came to another, he said to him: 'My master invites thee.' He said to him: 'My friend is to be married and I am to arrange a dinner; I shall not be able to come. I pray to be excused from the dinner.' He went to another, he said to him: 'My master invites thee.' He said to him: 'I have bought a farm, I go to collect the rent. I shall not be able to come. I pray to be excused.' The servant came, he said to the master: 'Those whom thou hast invited to dinner have excused themselves.' The master said to his servant: 'Go out to the roads, bring those whom thou shalt find, so that they may dine. Tradesmen and merchants shall not enter the places of my Father.'"

Scholars still debate whether the Gospel of Thomas is derived from our canonical gospels or represents instead an independent tradition of the sayings and parables of Jesus. It does seem that the latter is the best possibility at the moment. There is also a problem about whether Matthew and Luke have a common source or are mutually independent versions. For now, I shall leave aside these problems in source criticism and work with three variants of one original story. I shall be concerned with what that original story said and with what changes were effected in it and why. Even a cursory reading of the three versions given above discloses the general similarities and also the individual differences in the three accounts.

I have two reasons for spending so much time on this parable. First, it is a classic case of the tradition's change of a parable of Jesus into an *example-story* and an *allegory* of the history of salvation. If we understand this case, we will have grasped a process at work in all the parables of Jesus. Second, it is a somewhat amusing example of what happens when a parable is taken literally. Matthew finds he has to add a postscript to the story, warning that there might be some at the feast who would get thrown out by the master!

Invitation to first guests. The festive occasion has grown dramatically from a small dinner party in Thomas, to a great banquet in Luke, and into the wedding banquet of a king's son in Matthew. The degree of culpability on the part of the refusing guests is much greater in Matthew and Luke than in Thomas. In the first two cases they had accepted a past invitation but, upon being reminded of the present arrival of the date, they refuse to come. This makes their excuses sound like deliberate insults. But in Thomas the story is both simple and realistic. The man prepares a dinner and sends out invitations, apparently that very day. By the time the servant goes around to the guests and gets back with their refusals, the dinner is already prepared and will be wasted now that no one is coming. The refusals seem much less insulting and much more normal in Thomas.

Servant(s) and refusals. The most obvious difference is now between Matthew and the other two sources. Matthew sends out two groups of servants, and those in the second group are murdered; a lethal note enters the heretofore somewhat amusing story. Neither Luke nor Thomas has two groups of servants or, indeed, even one group. Each has a single servant going from one guest to the next, inviting them in turn. Both have the dialogue in direct speech between servant and guest. The only significant difference is that Luke has three refusing guests while Thomas has four excuses and refusals.

Punishment. Since Matthew alone has the murder of the servants, he alone has the punishment for this murder, and it involves the burning of the murderers' city.

Invitation to new guests. There are two major differences. Luke alone has two separate invitations to two groups of replacement, or new, guests. Second, Luke alone specifies the new guests as "the poor and maimed and blind and lame." Matthew has "bad and good" among them, but Thomas simply says "those whom thou shalt find."

Conclusion. The most striking difference is in Matthew. He alone has a whole new act in the drama, that of the wedding garment. Presumably it is because of this addition that he has made the banquet a wedding from the very beginning. But this incident does not fit well with the earlier story. When guests are gathered in from the streets without warning, it does not seem fair to expect sartorial elegance from them!

What do all these changes and differences mean? I would propose an original story which would have gone, in summary, like this: A man decided on a small dinner party. He sent his servant to invite three guests, and he made preparations for the dinner (to be held that evening). By the time the servant had gone to all the guests and returned with the bad news that all of them were otherwise occupied, the dinner had already been prepared. Exasperated, no doubt as much with himself as with his friends, the master sent the servant out to bring in anyone he could find. In this version we have the standard folkloric threesome as in, for example, Goldilocks and the Three Bears. Axel Olrik wrote a now classical article in which he said, "The Law of Three extends like a broad swath cut through the world of folk tradition, through the centuries and millennia of human culture. The Semitic, and even more, the Aryan culture, is subject to its dominant force. The beginnings of its rule are, in spite of all the recent excavations and discoveries, lost in the obscurity of prehistory."[7] So we have three guests in the original parable. What, then, happened to this earlier version? Two separated but inter-connected forces of transformation have been allowed to play upon it. It has been both moralized in the direction of an example or exemplary story and allegorized as an image of the history of salvation. I shall take these transformational processes one at a time.

Morality. In the case of Thomas the concluding statement, "Tradesmen and merchants shall not enter the places of my Father," makes the author's understanding of the story quite clear. This conclusion also explains why he would want to expand the number of refusing guests from the original three to four "tradesmen and merchants." Just as the businessmen of the story missed the dinner, so also such persons will not reach "the places of my Father." The story is a negative example, a story of how one is not to act. With Luke the story is also primarily an example, but the emphasis is on the positive side, on what one is to do. In the immediately preceding section in Luke 14:12–14 Jesus had said, "When you give a dinner or a banquet, do

7. Olrik, "Epic Laws of Folk Narrative," in Dundes, *Study of Folklore*, 134.

not invite your friends or your brothers or your kinsmen or rich neighbors, lest they also invite you in return, and you be repaid. But when you give a feast, invite the *poor, the maimed, the lame, the blind,* and you will be blessed, because they cannot repay you. You will be repaid at the resurrection of the just." Luke then inserted into the story of the Great Feast this listing (italicized above) of the social outcasts in 14:13. But the point is surely quite different in the two units. In 14:12–14 Jesus says not to invite one's friends but to invite the outcasts, in order to obtain heavenly rather than earthly return. The story would say, if taken as an example, "invite first your friends but, if they cannot come, then invite the outcasts so as not to waste the food." This makes it clear that Luke himself added the mention of "the poor and maimed and blind and lame" from 14:13 to 14:21 and thereby made of the story a positive example of how one should act.

Allegory. There may also be some implicit allegorizing in Luke's version of the story. He may have intended the first or refusing guests to be those in Israel who had not accepted Christ, while the new guests represented those in Israel who believed in Christ (those in "the streets and lanes of the city") and the Gentile believers as well (those in "the highways and hedges"). This is, in any case, a very slight allegorization compared with Matthew, where the allegorizing process is so heavy-handed that it renders the story somewhat incredible. The murderous refusal is narrative overkill, the punitive expedition "during" the feast is unlikely, and, as already seen, the wedding garment does not fit well with the preceding story. But all this is quite reasonable if we read the story as an allegory of the history of salvation, as Matthew sees it. It is then clear that parts of the story of the Great Feast have been influenced by the preceding story of the Evil Husbandmen in Matt 21:33–46.

Compare these verses for instance:

The Evil Husbandmen	*The Great Feast*
he sent his servants . . . he sent other servants (21:34, 36);	he sent his servants . . . he sent other servants (22:3, 4);
And the tenants took his servants and beat one, killed another, and stoned another (21:35);	while the rest seized his servants, treated them shamefully, and killed them (22:6);
He will put those wretches to a miserable death (21:41).	he sent his troops and destroyed those murderers and burned their city (22:7).

The lethal situation allegorized in the parable of the Evil Husbandmen has been allowed by Matthew to infiltrate the more domestic story of the Great Feast. But this renders Matthew's purpose clear. The story is an allegory of salvation history. Israel has not accepted the invitation to the banquet and has, for Matthew, killed the prophets who brought the invitation. Hence he has the servants in two groups, representing the earlier and later prophets. Israel, says Matthew, was punished by the destruction of Jerusalem in the year 70 CE But even within the Christian community Matthew finds "bad and good" present, and so he adds the wedding garment incident to warn that even some Christians might be rejected by God, that more is needed than mere presence within the Christian community. This reflects a problem within the Matthean community well known from many other places in his gospel. So, in summary, Matthew allegorized the story and Luke and Thomas moralized it. But the parabolic structure of the original story is still clear behind these changes, as figure 18 indicates. Or, as Jesus might have said, the

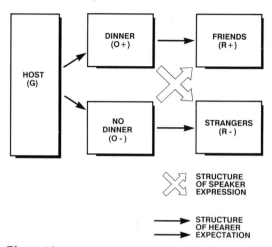

Figure 18

One expects a host to have his friends at dinner and not
strangers, but in the story strangers are present and friends
are absent, all quite plausibly.

kingdom of God will strike you as being as nonsensical as
a dinner with all one's friends absent and only strangers
present.

At this point I want to say to the Host of the Great Feast
as to the Doorkeeper of Kafka's story, "All this is quite,
quite impossible." But then I recall what Soren Kierkegaard said in his *Panegyric upon Abraham.* "Everyone shall
be remembered, but each became great in proportion to
his expectation. One became great by expecting the possible; another by expecting the eternal, but he who expected the impossible became greater than all. Everyone
shall be remembered, but each was great in proportion to
the greatness of that with which he strove."[8]

8. Kierkegaard, *Fear and Trembling,* 31.

97

Parable and Kingdom

These few examples of the parables of Jesus will have to suffice. The parable of the Great Feast was treated in some detail because it is a classical case of an original parable being transformed by the tradition towards moral example and historical allegory. Joachim Jeremias delineated very clearly these two major transformational processes at work in the parabolic tradition. But there is an element of unconscious irony running through his analysis. On the one hand, he carefully and correctly separates the moralizing and allegorizing additions made by the tradition and usually treats these additions with something less than enthusiasm; on the other hand, he all too often introduces very similar moralizing and/or allegorizing tendencies back into his interpretation of the original version. What goes out the text's door comes back in the interpretation's window.[9] But whether or not one agrees that most or even all of Jesus' stories were originally intended as parables, it is clear that the ones indicated in this chapter place Jesus squarely in the tradition of parable-teller.

I do not mean to claim any superiority for parables over examples or allegories. My aim in distinguishing these types is to show that in the change from parable into example-story and/or allegory a sea-change is effected, and one should not be surprised if the result is a rather forced example and/or a rather strained allegory. The point is not that there are examples and allegories in the gospels and that these are bad types of literature but that the examples and allegories in the gospels are bad members of these species; the main reason for their failure is not the literary incompetence of the evangelists but the

9. See Jeremias's magisterial work *The Parables of Jesus.*

98

difficulty, if not impossibility, of changing original parables into example-stories and allegories. Recall the typology given earlier in figure 4 and note how parable is quite
removed from apologue. Yet examples and allegories
would be subforms of apologue. To quote Sacks a final
time, "Christian allegories [are] a subclass of example or
apologue."[10] Parables are not "better" than examples or
allegories, they are simply different literary forms with
different functions. As a storyteller, Jesus was a parabler
rather than a moralist or an allegorist.

All of this leads to some very important conclusions
regarding the message of Jesus. Scholars generally agree
that Jesus proclaimed the "kingdom of God." What would
such as expression have meant to Jesus' audience? Norman Perrin states that "the primary and essential reference
is to the sovereignty of God conceived of in the most
concrete possible manner, i.e., to his *activity* in ruling. . . .
The Kingdom of God is the power of God expressed in
deeds; it is that which God does wherein it becomes
evident that he is king. It is not a place or a community
ruled by God; it is not even the abstract idea of a reign or
kingship of God. It is quite concretely the activity of God
as king."[11] The term "kingdom of God," then, places the
major emphasis on the act wherein and whereby God's
sovereignty is made manifest.

Scholars also agree that Jesus taught in stories. What is
the connection between these two points, the kingdom of
God and the stories of Jesus? I would suggest that the
connection is summed up in the maxim: Parables give God
room. The parables of Jesus are not historical allegories
telling us how God acts with mankind; neither are they

10. Sacks, *Fiction and the Shape of Belief*, 263.
11. Perrin, *Rediscovering the Teaching of Jesus*, 55.

moral example-stories telling us how to act before God and towards one another. They are stories which shatter the deep structure of our accepted world and thereby render clear and evident to us the relativity of story itself. They remove our defences and make us vulnerable to God. It is only in such experiences that God can touch us, and only in such moments does the kingdom of God arrive. My own term for this relationship is transcendence.

Perhaps it is only in moments of mortal jeopardy that this exclusion of security comes most deeply home to consciousness. At such times we best realize that security is the serenity that comes from accepting insecurity as our mortal lot. As in so many other matters, Shakespeare caught a glimpse of this problem long ago. In *King Richard II*, act V, scene 5, the king has been imprisoned by Bolingbroke and thinks,

> For no thought is contented. The better sort,
> As thoughts of things divine, are intermix'd
> With scruples, and do set the word itself
> Against the word:
> As thus, "Come little ones" and then
> again,
> "It is as hard to come as for a camel
> To thread the postern of a small needle's eye."

The "better sort" of thoughts, like those in the Bible, do not furnish easy assurance but challenge us with their contradiction even of each other.

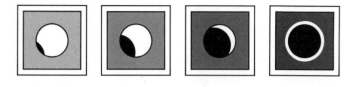

Epilogue:
The Parabler
Becomes Parable

Being now no more a singer but a song . . . .
Swinburne

I have interpreted the stories of Jesus as parables intended
to shatter the structural security of the hearer's world and
therein and thereby to render possible the kingdom of
God, the act of appropriation in which God touches the
human heart and consciousness is brought to final genu-
flection. I have also argued that the tradition of the primitive church changed these stories from parables into moral
examples or exemplary stories and/or historical allegories.
These latter described in story how God acts towards his
people and/or how they should act in response to him or
towards one another. In effecting this change the early
church moved these stories back into literary types well-
known from the carefully constructed pedagogical meth-
ods of the rabbis. I did not mean to imply, in describing
this process, that it was illegitimate or decadent transition
in itself. I did question, however, if they had always or

could ever succeed in making a smooth change from parable to example and allegory.

But what is most fascinating for me in this process of change from parables to examples and allegories is the phenomenon of human transformation going on before our eyes. And this gives rise to our final problem. How was it possible or necessary for this transformation to take place? How and why did the tradition change these stories from parables to examples and/or allegories?

My answer to this crucial problem of the transition from the message of the historical Jesus to the message of the primitive church is guided by this saying: The parabler becomes parable. Jesus announced the kingdom of God in parables, but the primitive church announced Jesus as the Christ, the Parable of God. Two examples of this transformation will be discussed.

Jesus had gathered around him a group of followers who had committed themselves deeply to his vision as a challenge from God. This decision had already involved them in severe tension with other groups within their religious community. And then Jesus was hung on a Roman cross, crucified as an insurgent against the imperial power. This execution may well have been triggered by a parabolic action in which he symbolically "destroyed" the Temple, bringing a parabolic *word* such as that of the Good Samaritan to its logical parabolic *deed*. But be that as it may, the followers had now to face the awful question: Had it all been some terrible mistake? Was this crucifixion the judgment of God against Jesus, the repudiation by God of Jesus' claims and assertions? Jesus had said that the kingdom would meet his followers where and when their world was overturned and challenged at its very depths. And they had nodded in agreement at this very interesting if somewhat abstract proposition. Now it had all come

home to them at last. There was the *Cross,* and the immediate conclusion was that it represented the divine rejection of Jesus. But if Jesus' parabolic vision was correct,
then the Cross itself was not rejection but was itself the
great Parable of God. Now, and probably only now, they
finally understood what Jesus had been telling them all
along. The Cross replaced the parables and became in
their place the supreme Parable. The parables themselves,
no longer the center, were freed to become examples and
allegories—otherwise they would probably have been lost
to us forever. All this Paul explained to the Corinthians,
who were much impressed by their own spiritual gifts of
speech and action:

> Where is the wise man? Where is the scribe? Where is
> the debater of this age? Has not God made foolish the
> wisdom of the world? For since, in the wisdom of
> God, the world did not know God through wisdom, it
> pleased God through the folly of what we preach to
> save those who believe. For Jews demand signs and
> Greeks seek wisdom, but we preach Christ crucified,
> a stumbling block to Jews and folly to Gentiles, but to
> those who are called, both Jews and Greeks, Christ
> the power of God and the wisdom of God. For the
> foolishness of God is wiser than men, and the weak-
> ness of God is stronger than men (1 Cor 1:20–25).

Instead of signs and wisdom, parables and Parable. So the
parables of Jesus became the examples and allegories of
the church, and the Cross of Jesus became the Parable of
the church. Jesus died as parabler and rose as Parable.

A second example is the creation of the gospel format
by Mark. Werner Kelber has argued that Mark was written
after the fall of Jerusalem in 70 CE to validate the parabolic
claim that Galilean Christianity, not Jerusalem Christian-

ity, was the focal point of obedience to God.[1] Once again, parable is renewed. God is not found where one would expect, with the relatives and disciples of Jesus in Jerusalem, but with the community of Jews and Gentiles in Galilee. David Hawkin summed up Mark's intention with these words:

> Mark's task as a writer is to introduce his readership to a new scheme of things, in which ordinary values are reversed and reasonable judgments disqualified. The destiny of Jesus is the paradigm of Christian existence. To "comprehend" is to discover and affirm the law of the cross as the supreme eschatological reversal. The dimensions of Mark's pedagogical task, then, are considerable. His strategy is to thematize incomprehension not only as superficiality and ignorance, but above all as that blindness that comes from the contradictions of human appearances and ambitions.[2]

Each time the Parable is in danger of becoming fossilized and turned into a myth, it subverts its own domestication and breaks the very structures that would contain it.

I would agree with Robert Frost against W. B. Yeats on this point. Yeats had argued in "Two Songs from a Play" that Jesus had introduced violence into the world against the toleration of Greek culture.[3] But Frost countered:

> [Yeats] charged the Nazarene with having brought
> A darkness out of Asia that had crossed
> Old Attic grace and Spartan discipline

1. Kelber, *The Kingdom in Mark*.
2. Hawkin, "The Incomprehension of the Disciples in the Marcan Redaction," 500.
3. Yeats, in *Collected Poems*, 210–11.

104

With violence. The Greeks were hardly strangers
To the idea of violence. It flourished
Persisting from Old Chaos in their myth
To embroil the very gods about their spheres
Of influence. It's been a commonplace
Even since Alexander Greeced the world.
'Twere nothing new if that were all Christ brought.
Christ came to introduce a break with logic
That made all other outrage seem as child's play:
The Mercy on the Sin against the Sermon.
Strange no one ever thought of it before Him.
'Twas lovely and its origin was love.[4]

People are fond of discussing two types of religion, historical and mythical, and of asserting that Judaism and Christianity are in the former category because they link their claims to the objective reality of certain key events. Maybe the time has come to retire this distinction as irrelevant and to replace it with another. The more useful distinction might be between mythical religion, a religion that gives one the final word about "reality" and thereby excludes the authentic experience of mystery, and parabolic religion, a religion that continually and deliberately subverts final words about "reality" and thereby introduces the possibility of transcendence.

Which do we prefer, comfort or courage? It may be necessary to make a choice.

---

4. Frost, in *Poetry*, 511.

Bibliography

Auden, W. H., *The Dyer's Hand and Other Essays*. New York: Random House, 1962.

——, *Collected Longer Poems*. New York: Random House, 1969.

Barrenechea, A. M., *Borges the Labyrinth Maker*. New York: New York University Press, 1965.

Barth, John, "The Literature of Exhaustion." *The Atlantic Monthly* 220 (August 1967):29–34.

Barthes, Roland, "Introduction à l'analyse structurale des récits." *Communications* 8 (1966): 1–27.

——, *Critical Essays*. Evanston, IL: Northwestern University Press, 1972.

Belitt, Ben, "The Enigmatic Predicament: Some Parables of Kafka and Borges." *Prose for Borges = TriQuarterly* 25 (1972): 269–93.

Borges, Jorges Luis, "Death and the Compass." Pp. 76–87 in *Labyrinths: Selected Stories and Other Writings*. Ed. D. A. Yates and J. E. Irby. New York: New Directions, 1962.

——, *The Aleph and Other Stories, 1933–1969*. New York: Bantam, 1971.

——, "The Analytical Language of John Wilkins." Pp. 101–5 in *Other Inquisitions 1937–1952*. New York: Simon & Schuster, 1964.

_____, "The Circular Ruins." Pp. 57–63 in *Ficciones*. New York: Grove 1962. = Pp. 45–50 in *Labyrinths. Selected Stories and Other Writings*. New York: New Directions, 1962. = Pp. 68–74 in *A Personal Anthology*. New York: Grove, 1967. = Pp. 34–40 in *The Aleph and Other Stories, 1933–1969*. New York: Bantam, 1971.

Brooke-Rose, Christine, *A ZBC of Ezra Pound*. Berkeley and Los Angeles: University of California Press, 1971.

Burgin, Richard, *Conversations with Jorge Luis Borges*. New York: Holt, Rinehart & Winston, 1968.

Dickinson, Emily, *The Poems of Emily Dickinson*. Ed. T. H. Johnson, 3 Vols. Cambridge, MA: Belknap Press of Harvard University Press, 1955.

Donahue, John R., "Tax Collectors and Sinners." *Catholic Biblical Quarterly 33* (1971): 39–61.

Dundes, Alan, ed., *The Study of Folklore*. Englewood Cliffs, NJ: Prentice-Hall, 1965.

Eissfeldt, Otto, *The Old Testament: An Introduction*. New York: Harper & Row, 1965.

Eliot, T. S., "A Commentary." *Criterion XII* (1932): 73–79.

_____, *Four Quartets*. New York: Harcourt, Brace and World, 1943.

_____, "Tradition and the Individual Talent." Pp. 259–66 in *Perspectives on Poetry*. Eds. J. L. Calderwood and H. E. Toliver. New York: Oxford University Press, 1968.

Fann, K. T., *Wittgenstein's Conception of Philosophy*. Oxford: Blackwell, 1969.

Frost, Robert, *A Collection of Critical Essays*. Ed. James M. Cox. Englewood Cliffs, NJ: Prentice-Hall, 1962.

_____, *The Poetry of Robert Frost*. Ed. E. C. Lathem. New York: Holt, Rinehart & Winston, 1969.

Frye, Northrup, *The Educated Imagination*. Bloomington, IN: Indiana University Press, 1964.

_____, "The Critical Path: An Essay on the Social Context of Literary Criticism." *Daedalus 99* (1970): 268–342.

Greimas, Algirdas Julien, *Sémantique structurale. Recherche de méthode*. Paris: Larousse, 1966.

Hawkin, David J., "The Incomprehension of the Disciples in the Marcan Redaction." *Journal of Biblical Literature 91* (1972): 491–500.

Hesse, Mary B., *Models and Analogies in Science*. Notre Dame, IN: Notre Dame University Press, 1966.

Janik, A., and S. Toulmin, *Wittgenstein's Vienna*. New York: Simon & Schuster, 1973.

Jason, Heddy, *Conflict and Resolution in Jewish Sacred Tales*. Ph.D. dissertation: Ann Arbor, MI: University Microfilms, 1968.

Jeremias, Joachim, *The Parables of Jesus*. Rev. ed. New York: Charles Scribners' Sons, 1963.

Kafka, Franz, "Before the Law." Pp. 61–79 in *Parables and Paradoxes*. New York: Schocken, 1961.

Kelber, Werner, *The Kingdom in Mark*. Philadelphia: Fortress Press, 1974.

Kermode, Frank, *The Sense of an Ending*. New York: Oxford University Press, 1967.

Kierkegaard, Soren, *Fear and Trembling & The Sickness Unto Death*. New Jersey: Princeton University Press, 1954.

Kirk, Russel, *Eliot and His Age*. New York: Random House, 1971.

Kuhn, Thomas S., *The Structure of Scientific Revolutions*. 2d ed. enlarged. Chicago: University of Chicago Press, 1970.

Leach, Edmund, *Genesis as Myth and Other Essays*. Cape Editions 39. London: Cape, 1969.

Lévi-Strauss, Claude, *Structural Anthropology*. Garden City, NY: Doubleday & Co. 1967.

———, *The Savage Mind*. Chicago: University of Chicago Press, 1970.

Maranda, Elli Köngäs and Pierre, "Structural Models in Folklore," *Midwest Folklore* 12 (1962):133–92; slightly adapted in *Structural Models in Folklore and Transformational Essays*. Approaches to Semiotics 10. The Hague Mouton, 1971.

Maranda, Pierre, ed., *Mythologies: Selected Readings*. Baltimore: Penguin, 1972.

McKenzie, John L., *A Theology of the Old Testament*. Garden City, NY: Doubleday & Co., 1972.

Miles, J., "Laughing at the Bible: Jonah as Parody." *The Jewish Quarterly Review* 65 (1975): 168–81.

Neruda, Pablo, "Autumn Testament." P. 405 in *Selected Poems*. Ed. N. Tarn. New York: Delta, 1973.

Nietzsche, Friedrich, *The Portable Nietzsche*. Ed. Walter Kaufmann. New York: Viking, 1970.

Perrin, Norman, *Rediscovering the Teaching of Jesus*. New York: Harper & Row, 1967.

Popper, Karl, *Conjectures and Refutations: The Growth of Scientific Knowledge*. London: 1963.

Pound, Ezra, *The Cantos of Ezra Pound*. New York: New Directions, 1972.

Ricoeur, Paul, "The Problem of the Double-Sense as Hermeneutic Problem and as Semantic Problem." Pp. 63–79 in *Myths and Symbols. Studies in Honor of Mircea Eliade*. Eds. J. M. Kitagawa and C. H. Long. Chicago: University of Chicago Press, 1969.

Rilke, Rainer Maria, *Selected Works: II. Poetry*. Trans. J. B. Leishman. New York: New Directions, 1967.

Sacks, Sheldon, *Fiction and the Shape of Belief*. Berkeley and Los Angeles: University of California Press, 1966.

Vail, L. M., *Heidegger and Ontological Difference*. University Park and London: The Pennsylvania State University Press, 1972.

Van Buren, Paul, *The Edges of Language*. New York: Macmillan, 1972.

Waismann, F., "Notes on Talks with Wittgenstein," *Philosophical Review* 74 (1965): 12–16.

Whitehead, Alfred North, *Process and Reality*. New York: Macmillan, 1969.

Williams, William Carlos, "An Approach to the Poem." Pp. 50–76 in *English Institute Essays, 1947*. New York: Columbia University Press, 1948.

Wittgenstein, Ludwig, *Tractatus Logico-Philosophicus*. London: Routledge & Kegan Paul, 1922.

Yeats, W. B., Pp 210–11 in *The Collected Poems of W. B. Yeats*. New York: Macmillan, 1956.

Supplemental Bibliography

Crossan, John Dominic, *In Parables: The Challenge of the Historical Jesus*. New York: Harper & Row, 1973; Sonoma, CA: Polebridge Press, 1990.

_____, ed., "The Good Samaritan." *Semeia* 2 (1975).

———, *Raid on the Articulate: Comic Eschatology in Jesus and Borges.* New York: Harper & Row, 1976; Sonoma, CA: Polebridge Press, revised edition forthcoming.

———, *Finding is the First Act.* Philadelphia: Fortress Press, 1979.

———, *Cliffs of Fall: Paradox and Polyvalence in the Parables of Jesus.* New York: The Seabury Press, 1980.

Funk, Robert W., *Language, Hermeneutic, and Word of God.* New York: Harper & Row, 1966.

———, ed., "A Structuralist Approach to the Parables." *Semeia* 1 (1974).

———, *Jesus as Precursor.* Philadelphia: Fortress Press, 1975; Sonoma, CA: Polebridge Press, revised edition forthcoming 1991.

———, *Parables and Presence. Forms of the New Testament Tradition.* Philadelphia: Fortress Press, 1982.

Kissinger, Warren S., *The Parables of Jesus: A History of Interpretation and Bibliography.* Metuchen, NY: The Scarecrow Press, 1979.

Perrin, Norman, "The Modern Interpetation of the Parables of Jesus and the Problem of Interpretation." *Interpretation* 25 (1971): 131–48.

———, *Jesus and the Language of the Kingdom.* Philadelphia: Fortress Press, 1976.

Scott, Bernard Brandon, *Jesus, Symbol–Maker for the Kingdom.* Philadelphia: Fortress Press, 1981.

TeSelle, Sallie McFague, *Speaking in Parables: A Study in Metaphor and Theology.* Philadelphia: Fortress Press, 1975.

Via, Dan O., Jr., *The Parables: Their Literary and Existential Dimension.* Philadelphia: Fortress Press, 1967.

Wilder, Amos N., *Early Christian Rhetoric: The Language of the Gospel.* Rev. ed. Cambridge: Harvard University Press, 1971.

Indices

801.9
C 951 LINCOLN CHRISTIAN COLLEGE AND SEMINARY 92840

Whitehead, Alfred N., 6f.
Williams, William Carlos, 24
Wittgenstein, Ludwig, 2,
    8–11, 12
Yeats, W. B., 104

Subjects
allegory, 95–97, 98–99
art, 6, 7–13, 14, 24
crucifixion as parable, 102–3
Ezra, 54f.
game, 3–5
God, 25–30, 31
gospel form as parable, 103–4
Gospel of Thomas, 90–92
language 2, 12f., 24–25, 28–29
    of poetry, 7f., 10f., 22f.
    of science, 10f.
limit, 1–30
myth, 31f., 32–37, 40–45
parable, 31f., 37–40, 40–45,
        chapters 4, 5
    crucifixion as, 102–3
    of deed, 71–74
    gospel form as, 103–4
    and humor, 74–82
    and kingdom, 98–100
    and word, 82–97
Pharisee, 82–83
positivism, 9
progress, 6, 13–19
publican, 72–74, 82–83
reality, 24–25
    objective, 5
    external, 5, 19–24
science, 6, 7–13, 17f.
sport, 4
story
    action, 41–45
    apologue, 41–45
    limit, 5–30
    master, 31
    satire, 41–45
structure, structuralism, 35–40,
    48–52, 55–56, 58–60, 75, 83,
    88, 97

tax collectors, 72–74, 82–83
transcendence, 24–30, 99f.
world, 42

Biblical References
Daniel
    4:10–12, 76
    4:11, 77
Ezekiel
    17:22–23, 76
    17:24, 77
    21:2–6, 75f.
    31:3, 77
    34, 81
Ezra 9:1–2, 55
Isaiah 40:10–11, 80f.
Jeremiah 23:1–4, 81
John 10, 78f.
Luke 17:6, 75
Matthew 21:33–46, 95–96
Nahum, Book of, 58f.

Parables and Parablers
Borges, Jorge Luis, 7, 48, 60, 63–
    67, 68f.
Good Samaritan, 85–88
    Luke 10:25–36
Great Feast, 88–97
    Matt 22:1–14
    Luke 14:16–24
    GThomas 64
Hidden Treasure, 80–82
    Matt 13:44–46
Jonah, Book of, 48, 55–60
Kafka, Franz, 48, 60–63, 68, 97
Lost Coin, 77–82
    Luke 15:1–10
Lost Sheep, 77–82
    Luke 15:1–10
Mustard Seed, 74–77
    Luke 13:18–19
Pearl, 80–82
    Matt 13:44–46
Pharisee and Publican, 82–84
    Luke 18:9–14
Ruth, Book of, 48, 51–55, 58

114

3 4711 00086 7707